FEAR IS A
CHOICE

FEAR IS A CHOICE

TACKLING LIFE'S CHALLENGES WITH DIGNITY, FAITH, AND DETERMINATION

JAMES CONNER

with Tiffany Yecke Brooks

HARPER

An Imprint of HarperCollins*Publishers*

HarperCollins books may be purchased for educational, business, or sales promotional use. For information, please email the Special Markets Department at SPsales@harpercollins.com.

FIRST EDITION

Library of Congress Cataloging-in-Publication Data

Names: Conner, James (James Earl), 1995– author. | Brooks, Tiffany Yecke, author.
Title: Fear is a choice : tackling life's challenges with dignity, faith, and determination / James Conner ; with Tiffany Yecke Brooks.
Description: First edition. | New York City : Harper, 2020. |
Identifiers: LCCN 2020010256 (print) | LCCN 2020010257 (ebook) |
ISBN 9780062938435 (hardcover) | ISBN 9780062938442 (ebook)
Subjects: LCSH: Conner, James (James Earl), 1995- | Football players—United StatesBiography. | Cancer—Patients—United States—Biography. | Christian life.
Classification: LCC GV939.C645 A3 2020 (print) | LCC GV939.C645 (ebook) |
DDC 796.332092 [B]—dc23
LC record available at https://lccn.loc.gov/2020010256
LC ebook record available at https://lccn.loc.gov/2020010257

20 21 22 23 24 LSC 10 9 8 7 6 5 4 3 2 1

FOR MY GRANDMAMA, RUBY CONNER,
WHO PASSED AWAY JUST AS I WAS FINISHING
THIS BOOK. SHE WAS ABSOLUTELY A WOMAN WHO
TACKLED LIFE'S CHALLENGES WITH DIGNITY, FAITH,
AND DETERMINATION, AND I WILL ALWAYS CARRY
HER LOVE AND HER EXAMPLE WITH ME.

CONTENTS

AUTHOR'S NOTE: KEEP GOING

My mom gently scratched my back through my T-shirt as I sat in the chemo chair, watching the IV bag *drip-drip-drip* into the line that ran to the port catheter in my chest. I was three treatments in, which was just enough to know that they were not going to be a cakewalk, with an end point that seemed impossibly far away.

Two thoughts echoed in my head. One was simply two words: *Keep going*—an order I often gave to my mind during difficult practices when my body wanted to throw in the towel. The other thought was what my mom was murmuring quietly and reassuringly, just as she had comforted me when I was small: "This will all be a distant memory someday soon."

* * *

A lot of people ask me how I managed to stay so positive through the ups and downs of my junior year at Pitt. The answer is complicated, of course, but the first thing I will say is that I *didn't* always stay positive. There were definitely times when I felt discouraged, defeated, and angry—I think that's only natural. It's important to remember that those emotions are totally normal and totally healthy responses, as long as you don't hang out there or wallow in your negative feelings. But it's unrealistic to imagine you won't ever feel them at all. If you are facing a major obstacle, show yourself a little grace to experience whatever it is that you are experiencing. Don't try to convince yourself that everything is great; you'll know you're lying. But also recognize that you have the power to choose your response to your emotions. Personally, I chose to lean into optimism whenever I could.

The second factor that helped me was staying firm in my faith that God was working in this situation, whatever the outcome, and trusting that He had a plan and a purpose behind everything.

The third thing was having a tremendous support team around me—family, friends, teammates, coaches, people at my treatment center, and even the community—to remind me why I was fighting and to lift me up on days when it all felt like too much.

And the final thing that kept me going was the promise that time marches on. As long as we don't give up, whatever we are facing right now will one day just be a memory. *This, too, shall pass.*

I don't know what you are facing or even why you picked up this book. Maybe you are facing a difficult time and you wanted some words of encouragement. Maybe you're reading this just for the football with no interest in the inspirational stuff; that's totally fine—

because whatever prompted your interest, one thing is guaranteed: adversity is part of life. Hard times are promised to all of us, and if you're not experiencing them at this moment, I hope that something in these pages stays with you for when you do face your own challenges. Even if everything is going perfectly smoothly right now, the good times won't last forever. The awesome thing is, the bad times won't last forever, either.

Whatever plan God has for your life, I hope you trust that you are exactly where you need to be, right now, in order to get to where He is calling you to be tomorrow, in a month, in a year, or ten years down the road. You are the only person who gets to decide how you and God will write your story, together. My prayer for you is that when difficulties come, you will remember that you create your own destiny with God by your side.

What's more, I want you to remember that your destiny touches more than just you. When you live beyond fear in the truth of who you really are, even in the midst of trying circumstances, you become an example to others and help them to live with the same courage and hope.

Keep going. Every year, every day, every minute. Just keep going. Someday, this will all be a distant memory, but what you do with the challenges you faced will leave a mark on this world.

INTRODUCTION

SEPTEMBER 5, 2015

The day that changed my life. It was our season opener against Youngstown State—a season I was certain would get me recognized by NFL scouts in time for the spring draft. Having been named ACC Player of the Year the previous season, I was in a prime position to make this my best year ever as a true junior. I felt untouchable, on top of the world. Nothing was going to bring me down. All the hard work, sweat, and tears I'd invested in my training was finally going to pay off.

I was on fire the first quarter, scoring two touchdowns and rushing for more than 70 yards. I couldn't have scripted a better way to begin our game. Going into the second quarter, I was pumped, ready to go into full beast mode. As I lined up for what was to be my second carry of the quarter, a fleeting thought passed through my mind. *The pro scouts are going to be watching,* I realized. *If they thought last season was good, just wait until they see what I've got this year.* I was already playing the highlight reel in my head.

As Chad Voytik, our quarterback, called the play, I pushed off. I got the handoff and ran to the right, rolling past one tackle and surging forward with the ball. *Let's give 'em what they want to see,* I thought. I felt light, slick, electric. Half a second later, I felt a lurch as a Youngstown lineman dove low, hugging my legs and bringing me down. There was a pop as I hit the grass. As loud as the stadium was, that tiny sound deafened my trained ears. *Oh, God,* I thought as I rolled over, holding my knee, *please don't let this be anything bad.*

The pain was searing, but there was no way I was going to let anyone see that. My knee felt like it was about to buckle, but I was determined to walk off the field on my own two feet, even if it meant limping. After all, the scouts were watching! And they would still be watching every time the camera cut over to me on the sideline icing my knee. All I could do was sit there with a poker face, pretending my knee wasn't on fire, pretending I wasn't consumed by panic. I couldn't let on that, deep down, I knew something was wrong.

"It's a torn MCL. I'm afraid you're going to be out for the rest of the season."

There they were—the words I spent the past twenty-four hours begging God *not* to let me hear. I had blown out my knee in the first game of the year. I found out after spending an excruciating night trying to tell myself the pain would pass and that I'd be back on the field the next week. But the doctor's words ripped through the exam room and hung there for a moment as I struggled to process what

I'd just heard. My great plan for a dominant year that would launch me into the NFL draft had suddenly vanished into thin air, along with any ambitions I had for setting records and making the kind of impact I'd always dreamed of making for my team.

I managed to hold myself together for about two seconds, and then I dropped my head into my hands and started to cry. All I had ever wanted to be was a football player; I didn't know who I was without the sport. There was a battle going on inside my head as I struggled to hold tight to my faith while feeling like God had just *completely* betrayed me. Everything I had ever worked for or cared about was yanked away in an instant.

Although I didn't know it at the time, there was a battle going on inside my body, too. Not long afterward, I found myself sitting in another doctor's office staring at the words "symptoms consistent with lymphoma"—white letters on a black background—as they glowed back at me from a computer screen while the doctor confirmed the results of my biopsy. It didn't seem possible. How in the world could I have gone from a tweaked knee to a cancer diagnosis in the span of only three months?

What had seemed like the worst moment of my life became one of my greatest blessings: the torn MCL *led* to the discovery of the cancer. All the broken pieces of my dreams now came together to reveal a bigger picture. The moment I learned I had cancer, I suddenly realized that this was the battle God had been preparing me to fight all along—that every setback, frustration, and heartbreak along the way was really a gift He had given me to get me to this place. The battle wouldn't be easy—it would be called something else if it were—but I knew that my story was leading to this moment. It was up to me whether I would fight back or give in to fear. I chose to fight.

FEAR IS A
CHOICE

CHAPTER 1

PERSPECTIVE IS POWER

My hometown of Erie is a place of diverse history, cultures, and people, but, like most of western Pennsylvania, life generally revolves around two things: steel and sports. I hear people describe Erie as "industrial" and "gritty," but it was never anything but beautiful to me. Many of my childhood memories feature the sun reflecting off the water of Lake Erie, and how bright the shimmering light made everything else look. There used to be a lot of manufacturing in Erie, but much of it has since moved out of state, leaving a number of pretty sizable vacancies downtown. Some people see that as depressing—symbolic of loss or decay. But as someone who grew up amazed by the size of those buildings and the important things

I heard they did—manufacturing heavy mining equipment and packaging for every product imaginable that shipped all over the globe—I don't see loss. I see a reminder of what Erie did to put its stamp on the world. I see a powerful symbol of how strong the city and its people are. And I see potential for the city to redefine itself in our changing world.

My point is, we can see the same thing but interpret it entirely differently. Some people see Erie as a ghost town haunted by its industrial past; I see a city of creative, vibrant, hardworking people. That was a lesson I learned very early on, even if I didn't realize it until much later: perspective is *power*.

The way you choose to view a situation colors everything else about it, from how you respond in the moment to the lessons you end up taking away from it. The same is true for our lives. The stories we tell ourselves set the stage for how we view everything that happens to us; the way we frame those stories and choose to learn from them is up to us.

One of the earliest ways I learned this was in the way my mom managed our family. If I had one word to describe my home growing up, it would be *disciplined*. With five boys in the house, things could have easily slipped into chaos, but my mom was a brilliant organizer, and she knew the way to keep us out of trouble was to keep us busy. Every week, she would walk around the house and make up a list of things that needed to get done: mopping, vacuuming, washing dishes, mowing the lawn, pulling weeds, scrubbing toilets. She would make a chart breaking everything out by name so each person knew exactly what his job was. We would get home from school and find a two-page list—front and back—filled with chores. Our names were highlighted and the list was color coded; there was no way you could pretend you didn't know something was your responsibility.

Our house was always incredibly clean because Mom made our chores nonnegotiable. Granted, my brother Michael and I would usually take our time dancing and laughing in our room when we were supposed to be cleaning, but we knew we eventually had to get the job done. We took turns keeping an ear out for our parents' car in the driveway; we would be horsing around in the living room, but the moment one of us heard them pull in, he'd shout, "They're home!" and we'd all jump up and immediately act like we were hard at work. Mom never fell for it, though. "I was gone two hours and the only thing that got dusted was a lamp?" she'd say. "Uh-uh. I'm not buying it."

Discipline was the foundation of my youth. I don't mean that my childhood was a series of punishments or that we were afraid of my mom and stepdad—the opposite, in fact. My stepdad was strict, but it was always with a view toward teaching us self-reliance. Sure, we got in trouble when we deserved it, but their discipline wasn't about trying to break our will or make us fear their authority. In fact, Mom could even be a bit of a pushover if we were extra sweet about our apologies. She likes to remind me that when I was little, I didn't just pout or apologize; I would hug her, tell her I was sorry about whatever I had done wrong, and then say, "I'll pray about that so I'll do better." She says I always seemed to have a sense of personal responsibility in my mistakes when I was a kid. My parents wanted to lay the groundwork for us to be reliable, functional adults, and that meant everyone had to help carry their own weight around the house.

My mom's method for building character clearly worked because teachers often commented on what good manners the Conner boys had. As the youngest, I was afraid they were going to be sick of us by the time I filtered through their classes, but, surprisingly to no one but me, my brothers actually set a really good precedent. At least, if any of my teachers felt any dread when they saw yet another Conner on their roll at the beginning of the year, they never let on.

Glen was the oldest Conner boy; he was named for our biological dad and was the tallest of all of us—and not just because he was the oldest. He hit six feet by his freshman year of high school and just kept growing. He was lean and lanky, but with massive shoulders; I think every basketball coach in town wanted to recruit him on physicality alone. Rich was a year younger than him and almost as tall. He was broader all around, though, and built more like a line-backer. Not surprisingly, Rich was a football stud. Michael was a year younger than Rich—three boys in three years—and he was a combination of the two older brothers. He was tall and lean, but incredibly jacked and incredibly strong. Michael had muscles most teenage boys don't even know exist. Then there was a three-year gap between Michael and me. Our stepbrother, Rico, was a couple of months older than me and a lot closer to me in size than our big brothers, and I was the youngest whichever way you cut it. If that's confusing to you, don't feel bad—it was a little confusing to us, too. The important thing was that we were all really close in age. Basically, there were five boys all within six years, one month, and twelve days of each other.

Amazingly, my mom found a way to make each of her sons feel special, loved, and celebrated as individuals.

My very first memory, in fact, is of my mom making me feel like the most important person in the world. She and my dad split up when I was a toddler, and for a few years, she was a single parent. Even so, she never let us see any kind of stress or strain. And that was true on the morning of my fourth birthday. I woke up early—the sky was barely starting to show the dawn breaking through—and I heard someone in the kitchen. I was too excited about my birthday to go back to sleep, and I wanted to find out what was going on downstairs . . . but I didn't want to get in trouble for being up when I was supposed to be in bed. As quietly as I could, I tiptoed down four steps; there was a point where I could look through the railing and see into the kitchen but could also dart back upstairs if I was caught. There was my mom with a spatula, frosting a huge chocolate cake. Mom's Spidey senses must have been tingling because she looked up, right at where I was sitting, and as we locked eyes, we both broke into huge grins. It's a simple memory, but it always stood out to me as a moment when I knew with complete and utter confidence that I was loved—and that was a feeling that never wavered.

Around that same time, my mom's friend and her family moved in with us while they were going through a tough time. They were there for about seven or eight months—just two single moms, each working hard to make ends meet for her four boys. You read that right: there were eight boys ranging in age from four to ten all living under one roof. I'm sure it was chaotic, but I remember it as an awesome kind of chaos. We played epic games of red rover and four-on-four football, with the teams always divided by family. I think the "My brothers and me versus your brothers and you" mindset actually helped lay the groundwork for my tight relationship with my brothers later. We've been an "us"—a unit, a team, a force to be reckoned with—for as long as I can remember. I can't recall a time when I didn't have that assurance that I would never have to face anything alone, and that shaped my perspective tremendously. I couldn't imagine a single scenario when I wouldn't have the support of my family right beside me.

Not long after that family moved out, Mom married Melvin, my stepdad, and we moved to a house on West Twenty-ninth Street, where I did most of my growing up. It wasn't particularly large—only about sixteen hundred square feet—but a huge portion of the backyard was a cement slab with a basketball hoop, so we thought it was the greatest place on earth. We spent countless hours out there playing every man for himself, two-on-two, or rotating in and out to keep numbers even if it was a weekend when Rico was visiting. As the youngest, I never could get a rebound, but I learned to make the most of every opportunity when I did get the ball.

We also had an old barber's chair in a corner of the basement by the washer and dryer, and we would all sit there while Michael cut our hair. Why we trusted him and why Mom let him have a clippers, I will never know, but apparently he wasn't half bad at it because we did that for years. Glen was the most adventurous of us, going from an afro to cornrows to dreads; Rich and Michael usually just wanted their hair cut low. But we spent hours in that basement lifting weights, cutting hair, and laughing together.

While we didn't go on any vacations or big trips growing up, the house on Twenty-ninth Street was everything we could have wanted—Glen and Rich in one room, Michael and me in another, Rico sleeping wherever he felt like when he visited. Why would you even *want* to travel when you had a home that awesome?

Because we were so close in age, it would have been really easy for my brothers and me to fight constantly or fixate on negative competition, but we actually had the opposite experience. We shared clothes, toys, rooms, friends, secrets, and hobbies. There were plenty of wrestling matches and arguments, as with any siblings, but we always made up the same day; we placed a lot of importance on the idea of never going to bed angry. I don't remember anyone ever telling us to do that; I think we just knew that our house was only so big, and you couldn't really avoid the other person, so it just made more sense to forgive them. That may have been a pretty simple perspective, but it is one that served us well. Forgiveness—both granting it and seeking it—became second nature to us, and I believe we are all better people for it.

I wish I could say that this stemmed from our faith, and maybe it did a little, but not in any way that we were conscious of. When I was growing up, most of our religious activity was just praying at mealtimes and bedtime. Whether it was dinner at home or out at our favorite Chinese buffet with our dad, we knew we needed to take off our hats and bow our heads before we started to eat. Before Mom tucked us in each night, we would say our prayers together. We didn't attend church regularly when I was younger, but I know it was important to both my parents that we have a sense of thankfulness and humility to frame our lives. It wasn't until I was in college that I really started to think more seriously about my beliefs. When I was a kid, I just knew God was watching and prayer was important; anything more—like "blessed are the peacemakers"— was beyond me. But even so, we all let one another off the hook eventually.

Of all my brothers, Michael and I probably fought the most. I felt like he always checked me a little harder or fouled me a little more blatantly. Once, he put me in a headlock for a solid twenty minutes. In retrospect, it may have been less, but I can't say for sure because time becomes difficult to judge when your big brother is cutting off the blood supply to your brain. Whatever the case, I was furious. Once my face wasn't purple anymore, I swore I was never going to speak to him again. But then, maybe an hour later, he came into our room and started talking like Steve Urkel from *Family Matters*. I tried to stay mad. I really did. But Urkel is my weak spot (don't judge me), and I started laughing despite my best efforts. That was usually how our fights ended: someone made someone else laugh, and all was instantly forgiven.

Another time, during the summer I turned fourteen, I was absolutely livid at Rico for wearing one of the new shirts I had received for my birthday and was saving for a special occasion. With as much as we shared, including clothes, there was a kind of sacredness to something that belonged to just one person. When I saw Rico coming downstairs with that shirt on, I just lost it. But a few minutes later, he quoted something I can't even remember now from a Martin Lawrence movie, and I started cracking up. All it took was a couple of lines from a dumb comedy and everything would be all right again. That was just how we operated: what we had in common and the laughter we shared always trumped whatever disagreements were between us. I think the world would probably be a whole lot better if everyone embraced that principle. I'm not saying Steve Urkel can bring about world peace . . . but I'm also not *not* saying that.

Our parents never forced us to make up; that was always something we just did on our own. My brothers all have really big hearts, and we all realized that whatever we were fighting about just wasn't a major deal in the big picture. Even as kids I think we all realized that our relationships with one another were more important than a T-shirt, a Spider-Man action figure, or a foul in backyard basketball.

Even if we argued at home, we stuck together. Whenever we went out into the world, we always joked that Glen played security detail. He was constantly scanning to make sure the area was safe and that there wasn't anyone who looked like trouble. He did that at the park, at the mall—anywhere we went, he was on the lookout. "Nothing bad will happen to you with me," he swore to us. And it never did.

The absolute trust I had in my brothers from an early age helped shape my generally optimistic view of the world. I believed nothing bad could happen to us because that was the promise they made. It was just that simple. We really had an "us against the world" mentality. My brothers will tell you that they could be kind of rough on me when we were little, but I never saw it that way. If I got bulldozed playing defense or sacked in a carry, it just meant I would try harder to stay on my feet the next time. I probably ended up with a few extra bruises, but if I *did* get hurt in a wrestling match or dogpile, I always tried to hide it so Mom wouldn't say they had to go easy on me. In fact, as Rich describes it, because we were so close in age, we were almost like a litter of puppies; they didn't really view me as their youngest brother so much as the smallest one of the pack. I may have been the runt, but I was never picked on.

Well, except for when they stole my chocolate milk.

Ridgefield Elementary School is closed now, but, for one crazy year, Glen, Rich, Michael, and I were all students there, ranging from kindergarten to fifth grade. Almost every day, one of my brothers would take my chocolate milk from me during lunch, but, truth be told, I was usually pretty happy to give it. To be five and have your big brother come over to chat with you in the cafeteria makes you pretty darn cool, even if he does swipe your milk carton when he leaves.

Ridgefield was a ten-minute walk from our house, and even though I complained about it when I was little—especially during the winter—I honestly credit my speed to the six years I spent building up my leg muscles in elementary school. In fact, just like every grandpa ever, when my future grandkids ask me about the secret of my success, I'll say, "It all started when I had to walk uphill both ways, in the snow, just to get to school." *Perspective.*

I started to realize I might have a real knack for athletics in fifth grade, when my rec league basketball team went undefeated in our tournament. You see, unbeknownst to me, I'd been practicing at a much higher level than my peers. Whoever installed the basketball hoop in our backyard cemented it in a few inches higher than the regulation ten feet. Years of playing with that nonregulation hoop (and against guys older than me) set me up to sink a lot of baskets in that elementary school tournament. It's funny how the things that challenge you as a kid can actually prepare you for life later on. For a long time, I didn't even realize that the hoop at home was actually more difficult than the one I would shoot on at school; it was just what I knew, and I adapted myself to play to those parameters. I was overprepared in the best possible way, which gave me a huge boost in confidence. Rich still laughs about the fact that it wasn't uncommon for me to score 30 or 40 points in a game because, for the first time in my life, I was facing a lower hoop and kids who weren't a foot taller than me. I still have the little trophy I earned in that fifth-grade tournament.

In fact, I loved competition so much that one Saturday morning when Michael's eighth-grade Upward Sports basketball team was short a player, Melvin looked over at me where we were sitting in the bleachers and asked, "Do you want to give it a try?"

"Do you think I can?" I asked.

He shrugged. "You won't know unless you try."

So I volunteered to play and the other team agreed because, after all, how much of a threat could a fifth grader really be to a bunch of thirteen-year-olds? And that was how I became a youth league basketball ringer. Maybe playing against kids three years older would have seemed daunting to some ten-year-olds, but to me, it was totally normal. In fact, I was relieved I was out there with guys *only* three years older than me. I had already been making layups for a year because that was the only way to keep pace with my high-school-age brothers. Every Saturday morning, I prayed that Michael's team would be a player short so I could substitute in, and at least half the time, I did. I guess it's not a great testament to the commitment of Erie's youth to their middle school rec league sports that there were open spots almost every game, but I didn't mind at all. From my perspective, it just meant I was getting even more practice against tougher competition. There was no way that wasn't going to make me better.

If it had been up to me, I would have stayed with basketball and nothing else, but my mom had a different idea. In fifth grade, she signed me up for football with the Millcreek Youth Athletic Association to keep me out of trouble and to get my excess energy out because, let's be honest, the woman was trying to keep five boys from tearing the house down. I was incredibly nervous about learning a new sport and didn't want to play, but I toughed out the season, figuring that would make her happy and I'd never have to hit the gridiron again. Then, the following season, she told me she was planning to sign me up for football once more.

"I don't want to play this year," I told her.

"I think you should," she replied.

"Nah."

A week later, I found out she had signed me up anyway, and I was furious. Coach Keith Kaschalk would call the house, and if I recognized his number on caller ID, I just didn't answer the phone. I had no interest in football. Glen and Michael played basketball all four years of high school, and I was convinced that was my game, too. Only Rich had been a football player, and he was built a lot bigger than the rest of us—a huge, jacked offensive lineman.

Finally, between Mom's insistence and the coach's persistent phone calls, I reluctantly agreed to play again—or, more accurately, Mom dragged me to practice and made me get out on the field. I *dreaded* it. Football was so much more physically punishing than basketball, and there was a much higher chance of injury. I recalled worrying myself sick before each game the previous season, and I had no interest in going through that again.

I didn't admit it to my mom at the time, but that season ended up changing everything for me. There wasn't one big moment where I suddenly fell in love with the game, but the gridiron just grew on me, as if each grass stain and spot of mud on my uniform after a game also left a little imprint on my soul. As I started to understand the strategy of football more fully, I began to appreciate the nuances of the game in a different way. As my appreciation for the game grew, so did my body's natural response to it. I suddenly developed a spin move that made me almost untacklable. It wasn't anything I gave conscious thought to, but as I felt a guy grab me, my instincts took over. Suddenly, I moved in such a way that his hands couldn't hold on to me, and I took off down the field.

That was pretty cool, I thought as I ran the ball into the end zone after I made my first spin move. *I need to try that again next time.* Before I knew it, I began to love football.

I loved it even when my best friend Sean Gallagher's team (the Edinboro Scots) beat mine (the Coca-Cola Crush) and Sean knocked me down during the game. He still swears that he just slipped in the cold mud of the field, and that he wasn't actually *aiming* for my knees . . . but this is *my* story and I still say it was a dirty hit. I recovered, of course, and the following year we were on the same football team instead of opposing ones.

Sean and I have what I consider to be the best kind of friendship. Everything is a competition between us—sports, video games, eating, tattoos. You name it, we will try to outdo one another. Every event is like Game 7 of the World Series, but the moment the game is over, we're brothers again. (Sound familiar?) Besides building up strength walking to school and constantly competing against my big brothers, I think it was my friendship with Sean that had the biggest impact on how I developed as an athlete growing up. We challenged one another to be better and, as a result, we both improved.

I met Sean in fifth grade. His dad, Mike Gallagher, was the local sports reporter for WJET-TV in Erie, and he used my brother Michael in some of his commercials. I went along to see one of them being filmed, and that's where I met Sean. He went to a different elementary school than me, but we clicked instantly. He was one of the reasons I was most excited for sixth grade, because we would be attending the same school.

When I started at Walnut Creek Middle School, I had no idea that it would impact me as deeply as it did. I have a lot of fond memories from that school, even if I wasn't one of those kids who made honor roll every grading period or won all of the academic awards each year. Homework was a struggle for me, and I hated most of my classes except for PE. But all of the people at the school were really wonderful. The teachers, the principals, the lunch ladies—they all loved my brothers, and as they got to know me, they loved me, too. It's pretty incredible what a difference a supportive environment can make for a child in terms of what they remember. I might not have enjoyed being in school from a homework perspective, but I sure enjoyed going there from a social one.

My favorite memories from that age, though, are of playing sports. Starting in seventh grade, we were able to play football for the school, and that was when Sean and I became an incredible team. That first year, we were both running backs, but then Sean switched to quarterback in eighth grade and I was the starting running back; we played those positions together all the way through high school. I think the coaches were both impressed and annoyed with how well we read each other.

Sean was one of those kids who matured early. He was the first boy in our grade to hit his growth spurt and develop actual muscles—and not just the puny things the rest of us tried to convince ourselves were there when we flexed our arms. His nickname was "Mr. NFL," which made me want to earn an awesome nickname for myself. Whenever we divided into teams for backyard football games, in an effort to make things fairer, our friends would never allow us to be on the same side. Rather than being annoyed by this, Sean and I played even harder to outdo the other one. Bragging rights were a strong motivator in our friendship.

I also continued to play basketball, which was where I met my other best friend, Carson Lewis. Carson, Sean, and I became an unstoppable trio. Every day with Carson was a mix of two things:

we were either cracking up at each other's jokes (he claims that I have the loudest laugh he's ever heard from an otherwise quiet person) or we were trying to thrash the other person in whatever stupid competition we had decided was the most important thing in that instant.

Sean, Carson, and I spent weeks at each other's houses. The Gallaghers were basically my extended family—six more siblings and two additional parents. Sean felt the same way about my family. As far as we were concerned, it was the more, the merrier. How boring to only have one quiet house when you could have two or three loud, crazy places to enjoy? We would eat, sleep, and do our homework until one of our moms came and dragged us back home. To some people, the relaxed boundaries might have seemed chaotic, but to us, it was the beauty of doing life alongside people. We were totally open and honest about who we were—no one felt a need to put on airs or make a fuss out of "hosting." I will always carry with me the perspective I gained regarding the beauty of basic, honest authenticity and how it creates a comfortable home. Transparency generates trust, and trust is key for any relationship—in life or on the field.

My mom put a lot of emphasis on transparency, too. She was open with us kids about her mistakes. She got pregnant with Glen in high school and moved into her first apartment on her own at sixteen. Though she never regretted having kids, she also knew how much harder things were for all of us because of how young she was, and she encouraged us to make better decisions for our futures. She and my dad got married, finished school, worked multiple jobs, and did everything in their power to make sure that their boys would grow up feeling supported, loved, and safe. But Mom also impressed upon us the importance of making the best choices we could with respect to our futures. She never complained about how tough it was; she just put her head down and pushed forward. She always made sure we knew we were the most important thing in the world to her, and she wanted to set the right example of hard work. I had a front-row seat to the challenge of making ends meet and the difficult decisions between buying us new coats and paying the rent. I am grateful for those hard times and the lessons I gained from them because they gave me an appreciation for the little luxuries of life—like a chocolate birthday cake when I was four or fees for extracurricular sports. Mom may have done some things wrong in her life, but she did a whole lot more right.

I think her tenacity is especially impressive when you consider that my mom is only five feet four, and all of us were taller than her by the time we were in seventh grade. Even so, she ran a tight ship. You know you're up against a force of nature when someone that size can put the fear of God in the hearts of a bunch of huge teenage boys. It's funny, because Dad isn't particularly tall, either, so whenever someone asks us where our height comes from, Rich usually just shrugs and says, "Lots of fish sticks?"

Food was always something of a battlefield in our house, not because there was not enough of it but because Mom cooked the healthiest food we could buy in bulk, and we bought boring cereal. We wanted the good stuff with marshmallows and cool prizes inside, but instead we ended up with family-size boxes of bran flakes and toasted oats.

"We're not buying any more cereal until all this is gone," my step-dad would say, so we would reluctantly finish those boxes in the hope that we'd find Lucky Charms on the table the next morning. Instead, another box of healthy, tasteless cereal waited for us when we came downstairs for breakfast.

As a result, when my older brothers started their first jobs, we were really excited if they got hired at a restaurant. We finally had an in to the good stuff! Glen's first job was at Perkins and Rich's was at Applebee's. One of the biggest treats was when they called to ask if I wanted them to bring anything home; my request was almost always the same: boneless wings. Even now, as an adult, they taste like pulling one over on Mom. I try to keep really strict tabs on my diet to make sure that I am maintaining my best physical health, so a little indulgence like that still feels like a big deal.

I think I get that love for good food from my dad.

My biological dad didn't live with us during most of my childhood, but he was involved in our lives and made a lasting impression. Every time we slapped five before he pulled me into a hug or when we wrestled on the living room floor, I was amazed at the strength in his hands. He was an extremely hard worker, always picking up extra shifts at the restaurant where he was a cook, which meant he wasn't around for us as much as he would have liked to have been. When I was little, my parents even had their own restaurant called KG's—Kelly and Glen's—but Dad shut it down after they split and went to work for a major restaurant chain to make sure there was enough money for all us boys. He ended up working there for more than thirty years.

My biological dad's parents, whom we called Granddaddy and Grandmama, were quite a bit older than my mom's parents, and our time at their house was like a step back to a different generation—in all the best ways. We tended to do the big holidays at their house, which was always crammed full of aunts and uncles and cousins and every different type of food you could imagine. When it came time to eat, we would all hold hands in a chain that wound through the whole house, and Granddaddy would start into the blessing, asking God for health for every member of the family and thanking Him for all of the amazing food. Those prayers could last fifteen minutes or more, which feels like an eternity when you're a hungry kid. My brothers and I inevitably got to a point where we would start squeezing each other's hands as if to say, "Man, this prayer is getting long!" but it was also a beautiful pause to stop and really celebrate the people we loved and the incredible gifts we'd been given in this life. Once we started eating, the conversation was all laughter and jokes. The love in that house was so real; it was as much a part of the holidays as the smell of the turkey or the steam rising off of the greens.

Grandmama also loved to pull out old photo albums and teach us about our family history. She wanted to make sure we had a strong sense of who we were, who we came from, and what it had taken to get us to where we were. We knew Jesus was going to find his way into the conversation because he was pretty much just another family member. He was like an extra uncle—Grandmama's favorite—who was mentioned at every meal and in every conversation. My grandparents never lost sight of God's presence in their lives and everything He had done for them, and for all of us. They viewed everything through a lens of blessings and gratefulness, and encouraged us all to do the same. Their example of placing faith first and family at the forefront—the idea that when I put on a jersey that reads "Conner" across the back, I am representing all of us—stays with me to this day.

I've always been grateful that I grew up with grandparents who were a real and active part of my life. Both sets were completely different, but they were both incredibly good to us. We loved the special routines we could always look forward to at my dad's parents' house, but we also enjoyed the casual fun of my mom's parents as well. They were let's-grill-out-by-the-swimming-pool-and-just-see-where-the-day-takes-us people. We always had a blast at their house because they were so relaxed and mellow that nothing really seemed to faze them. A bunch of loud boys who could empty a fridge in five minutes flat? No big deal. That's what Grampa and Grammy's house is for. They always came through with exciting Christmas gifts to help make the holidays a little more special when we were kids, too. Moncy was tight at home, but Grampa and Grammy got us a video game system to share and always made sure we had new games under the tree. And do *not* get in their way when they are cheering on their teams. No fans are more loyal than my mom's parents, and they made sure we knew they were in our corner.

It was really helpful for me to have a chance to experience different types of homes and traditions growing up. I had one pair of grandparents who were more traditional and another who were more relaxed. Being biracial myself, I don't identify exclusively with one culture or another; I know that my family is a complex tapestry of cultures, stories, struggles, and hopes. I think that helped shape my perspective on life as much as anything else. One of the most beautiful things in the world to me is the fact that we can be shaped by where we came from but we still get to choose who we become.

As we got older, I realized that there was a lot I could learn from watching my brothers besides just how to do a layup on the court or make a faster cut on the field. Glen had the most amazing confidence and resilience; when he started training as a cage fighter when he was nineteen and I was thirteen, everything about the way he carried himself communicated an unshakable belief in himself and his toughness. I wanted that. Rich always emphasized the fact that lots of people have NFL talent, but lots of people *don't* have NFL drive, NFL discipline, and NFL passion. "Ability can only take you so far," he would tell me. "Responsibility for yourself and your role on the team make the real difference between a casual player and a true athlete." And Michael was a fiery study in contradictions. He was a world-class trash-talker on the basketball court, but when I watched the way he treated his girlfriends with respect and gentleness, I knew that was the kind of guy I wanted to grow up to be.

I also gained perspective from the friends my brothers spent time with and the choices they made about school. Being the youngest, I had an advantage in that way; Glen jokes that I got to take the best from each of them without picking up the bad habits like skipping school or shrugging off motivation. I watched the consequences of their actions play out, whether it was getting into trouble for running with the wrong crowd or getting more solid job opportunities after graduation because they applied themselves in school.

I remember visiting their first apartments when they were each on their own and realizing just how little they had. Obviously, most people don't have a lot when they are just starting out at eighteen, certainly not what they can expect to have at thirty-eight or sixty-eight, but the fact that money was so tight they could only go grocery shopping one day at a time surprised me. I'd only ever thought about the freedom of living alone, not the limited opportunities for people with only high school diplomas and no further training. They've all done pretty well for themselves since then, but at the time, I was sobered by the reality of their situations and committed myself to earning a scholarship to college however I could. Because I had the chance to watch them each take a different direction, I had the advantage of being able to make the best choices for myself without quite so much trial and error. That's not to say that every lesson stuck and I never made any mistakes myself—*ha!*—but having the opportunity to weigh my options after seeing various outcomes was hugely beneficial in keeping me a little closer to the straight and narrow than I might otherwise have been. That perspective prepared me for adulthood as much as any life-skills class I ever took in high school.

I credit a lot of that to my friends, too. From an early age, my parents and grandparents stressed to us the importance of picking the right group of people to hang out with. "You can be kind to everyone," they would say, "but make sure you're spending the most time with people who are going in the same direction you want to go."

That lesson stayed with me. I started looking around, watching the kids who stayed out of trouble and were respectful of our teachers and coaches. In fact, I think community sports was one of the best possible ways for me to start cultivating a friend group very deliberately. I got to know kids from other elementary schools when I was playing in Millcreek Youth Athletic Association football, which allowed me to start middle school already knowing who some of the good eggs were—kids like Sean and Carson. The same was true for high school; because I'd had a chance to meet kids from the other middle schools that fed into McDowell High School, I started with a good sense of who I could trust to be a good influence and who might tend to gravitate toward trouble. It felt like I had more confidence in making sure I had a solid friend group.

But even when my brothers and I screwed up, my parents were great about making sure we knew that love was not conditional on success or good behavior. They encouraged us to think about hard life lessons as part of the process of growing up and getting wiser, as well as our responsibility to God: we would learn, we would be forgiven, and we would try to do better next time.

Of course, as a kid, I didn't realize how valuable all those lessons in perspective would prove to be. I just knew that I felt loved and supported in every aspect of my life, and I knew that I had a choice in the way I responded to my circumstances. I could either be a victim—always feeling put out, picked on, and pushed around—or I could be a victor, watching my brothers and learning from their mistakes as well as their successes. I didn't always make the best choices, but I knew it was up to me to decide what to make of each experience that came my way.

I also know that growing up in a house of amazing athletes only made me better because they challenged me to bring my A game each day. Our competition with one another was never stronger than our love for one another, and I think that made all the difference. I came to love sports because I loved my brothers, and our years of playing together as kids is what paved the way for me to play at an elite level.

I had amazing family and amazing friends, and together they helped me realize that life really is whatever you make of it. It's more than just being an optimist and hoping things fall your way. How you choose to view a situation matters, but how you choose to *engage* the problem is what really makes the difference in the long run. It's easy to cry that the game is too tough or the competition is too big or the job is too hard. It takes courage to jump in the game and give it whatever you've got anyway.

As Rich said recently, life has never been fair to me. As the littlest brother, I was always fighting a bigger fight than the people around me. But I just always counted myself lucky that I got to play up to whatever challenge was put before me. If everything had been easy or fair, I probably would have believed I was entitled to a simple, easy path. Instead, I developed grit.

It was that resilience and resourcefulness that set me up to face the experiences and opportunities that would arise in my health and career down the road. There was no way I could anticipate exactly what was coming, but the lessons in perspective from my youth prepared me to tackle every situation with optimism, determination, and a sense of coming out better on the other side.

CHAPTER 2

BE WILLING TO BE HUMBLED

The tissue paper of the shoebox crinkled as I folded it back and stared in disbelief at the gorgeous white cleats inside. These custom shoes were uniquely designed for my feet, with a bold "King James" scripted in navy blue across the back. "Whoa," I finally breathed.

My brother Rich patted me on the shoulder. He'd just gotten off his shift at Applebee's, and the grease from the fryer that clung to his shirt briefly overpowered the smell of new leather. "All right, J," he smiled. "You gotta ball now that I got you these."

But let's back up for a minute. To truly understand the significance of these cleats, you first need to know that we were a strictly generic-brand family. We rarely had a chance to get the "good stuff" (aka name-brand products) except for when there was a massive sale. When I lay in bed at night, dreaming about one day playing in the NFL, I did not imagine a life of limousines and posh nightclubs. Instead, the scene I played over and over in my head was of me strolling into Walmart, heading straight to the soap aisle, and picking out whatever body wash I wanted, *without* checking the price first. To me, that degree of freedom would mean that I had truly "made it."

As I held that pair of $130 custom shoes in my hand—shoes my brother had worked overtime to help me purchase—I knew that I had to make sure that his investment wasn't for nothing.

Over the years, I've had a number of teammates who had to fight their way up from painful circumstances like hunger or parents with addictions, so I recognize that my life was not as tough by comparison. But we did struggle. There were several years of food stamps and free lunches at school. College was just a pipe dream. My mom used to pray that if I could just get a partial scholarship to a junior college, she would exhaust herself trying to figure out how to get a loan for the rest. She would make sure I had my shot at a better future. Glen became the man of the house, taking on extra shifts to help buy school clothes for Michael and me.

My whole family was invested in seeing me succeed, which meant every time I was tempted to quit, every time I got fed up with how hard something was, every time I was faced with a choice, I knew there was more riding on it than just my own goals and ambitions. As a result, I pushed myself even harder.

Sometimes, the extra effort paid off; other times, it threatened my whole career.

When I look at my family, I can see how the character and talents

I developed as I grew up were a group effort. As my brother Michael says, we are all the product of one another—we all influenced, shaped, and challenged each other within our little family unit. We continually poured into the lives of everyone else around us. Mom absolutely dedicated herself to molding us into the kind of men she wanted us to become—kind, trustworthy, strong, sensitive, responsible, respectful, and hardworking. In fact, strangers used to stop her when we were out and about to compliment her on what a good job she was doing with the undoubtedly exhausting job of raising a bunch of small boys. We have become the people we are because of my mom's tireless efforts to keep us in line and out of trouble.

The same thing is true with my siblings. We shaped one another with the way we shared goals and love with each other. As Rich says, when you meet one brother, you are meeting all of us. There was never any jealousy between us—one person's success was everyone's success. As the youngest, I think I benefited the most from all of that; my brothers seemed especially dedicated to helping me go as far as I possibly could.

I remember seeing my brothers stand on the sidelines by the end zone, waving me down the field during my middle school games. One time I remember specifically, we were down 28–7 late in the fourth quarter. I broke a run to my left and about 10 yards in, I spotted them at the end of the field, reeling their arms and hollering, "Come on, J!" At the sight of my big brothers standing there, I shifted into the next gear and took off toward them—another 40 yards or so. We still lost, but I loved knowing that I had played all out to the final whistle, and my brothers had been there to see it. In fact, whenever our team went over to the high school to watch the older kids practice, I would beam from ear to ear whenever one of my brothers made a good play. I knew I was one of the luckiest kids in Erie; who else had heroes at home who were also heroes on the high school gridiron and the hardwood?

Michael used to sit me down and give me man-to-man talks about keeping my head on straight whenever he saw me slacking off or not being as dedicated to my work ethic as I should be. I think he felt an extra kind of responsibility, especially after Glen and Rich finished school and moved out ahead of us. Michael and I got especially close when it was just the two of us, playing football for hours on our asphalt basketball court and tackling each other whenever we could—in the grass, on the sidewalk, or at our grandparents' pool. He told me later he used to watch me play and would pray, *God, please let my little brother be stronger than me. Please let him be faster than me. Please give him a chance.*

But when it was finally my time to shine, I found it wasn't going to be quite as straightforward a path to the spotlight as I'd hoped.

In high school, I played on the freshman team, and I spent a lot of time figuring out what I could do with a body growing way faster than I could keep up with. Fourteen has got to be one of the weirdest ages for boys; there were some guys on the team who were probably still playing with G.I. Joes at home and others who already had legit mustaches. I was somewhere in the middle, but I was filling out quickly and getting fast. By my sophomore year on JV, I started to catch the eye of the varsity coaches, and I was sure that my junior year would be my breakout season.

Except that it wasn't.

A senior named Greg Garmon was on the roster ahead of me at running back. He had lost his home to a house fire at age six and had been diagnosed with cancer at age fourteen, but he fought his way back through all of that adversity to become the tenth-ranked high school running back in the *nation*, with offers pouring in from major Division I universities: Michigan, North Carolina, Virginia, Illinois, Iowa. While I respected the guy, I simultaneously felt a lot of frustration that he was taking the spotlight during what I believed was supposed to be *my* breakout season.

As Greg tore up the field, I was mostly relegated to blocking and didn't get the ball nearly as much as I would have liked. It didn't matter how hard I pushed myself in the weight room or on the field, I never could crack the top of the depth chart. Midway through the season, I'd only chalked up 15 or 20 carries total. "You'll get your shot next year," people assured me, but I knew that next year would be too late. College coaches start looking for recruits long before their senior year, and no one even knew my name.

When a defensive end got injured halfway through my junior season, my coaches asked me to make the switch. Finally, after talking it over with my brothers to make sure they didn't think I was shooting myself in the foot, I agreed. It was a deeply humbling move because I had always seen myself as a running back. To a nonsports person, that may sound a bit dramatic, but to anyone who has a deep love and devotion to a specific position, a change like that can really shake you up and affect how you understand your place on the team and in the game.

Ultimately, though, I had to ask myself what was more important to me: my identity as a running back or my chance to catch the eye of a college coach. When I weighed my options, I knew I had to play the long game, so I bit the bullet, made the switch, and learned the playbook from the other side of the ball.

The first time I attempted to put those new defensive skills into play was a Wednesday, just two days before Game 5 of our season. Chris Spooner, my defensive line coach, told me later that when he watched me get down in my position, he was completely confounded—it looked nothing like a normal defensive stance. I was low to the ground, nearly lying on my stomach, my legs stretched out behind me. It was ridiculous, frankly, but I had no clue what I was doing, so I adjusted my body into what I thought was the best posture for pushing off, and when the whistle blew, I charged. "He looks like a panther ready to pounce," Coach Spooner remarked to the head coach, Mark Soboleski, shaking his head. "I'm not sure he's going to start, but he's definitely going to play."

So there it was: I may have been humbled by giving up my position at running back but, as it turns out, humble pie can actually be pretty sweet. I discovered that in my very first game on defense, a game against Pine-Richland, a school in the suburbs north of Pittsburgh.

"Conner keeps running the wrong way," an outside linebacker complained to Coach Spooner. Coach called me over to the sideline.

"What are you doing?!" Coach Soboleski demanded, waving his clipboard as he charged at Coach Spooner and me.

"I'm reexplaining the strategy to him," Spooner explained.

"I don't care about that—just get Conner back in the game!" Soboleski yelled. "He's making tackles! I want him back in the game. Tell the other guys to adjust."

"You heard Coach," Spooner called in our next huddle. "Try to stick to the playbook, but if James runs right, you run left."

I may not have figured it all out before the end of the game, but whatever we did worked because I managed to sack the quarterback twice in that game. The first time I took him down, I thought, *This feels almost as good as a touchdown. I want more of these.*

By the end of the year, I not only got my defensive timing down, I also managed to break a school record. The previous benchmark had been 11 sacks in a season; I managed to rack up 12 sacks in only five and a half games. I'm not sure if I managed to make any college scouts sit up and take notice, but I know I definitely caught the eye of my high school coaches.

Just as my junior year ended, Coach Spooner invited me to come along with a group of players who were headed to a camp sponsored by the University of Pittsburgh.

Over the past few summers, my mom or coaches had taken me to several different daylong football camps in the area in the hope that I would end up on a few college coaches' radars. I attended camps hosted by Michigan State and Bowling Green. I was also really interested in Ohio State and USC, since a few players from our rival high school had been recruited there. Ultimately, though, we knew it would all come down to who noticed me and made an offer. High school recruits are ranked from one to five stars in terms of how competitive they are, and I was considered a two-star guy— basically, I was considered a prospect but not necessarily one major schools would end up fighting over.

The personal challenge, of course, was that the cost of those camps added up, and here I was looking at yet another one for Pitt—this time, it happened to be $50 per player to cover the cost of the van rental and registration. I was reluctant to ask Mom or my brothers to spot me yet again.

Whenever Mom drove me, we did everything on as tight a budget as we could manage, packing our lunches for the road and parking farther away in public lots to avoid higher fees. Things had gotten even tighter since she and my stepdad divorced. My brothers pitched in to help buy my school supplies and clothes—especially since most of their hand-me-downs were in pretty rough shape by the time they reached their fourth wearer—but we were still on a very strict budget. Fifty bucks was more than we were used to shelling out, but I also knew this summer was my last chance to get my name out there before my senior year began.

After dinner one night, I took a deep breath and asked Mom if I could have the money for the camp. She looked at me with raised eyebrows. "Really? That's a lot for a football camp."

"If I impress the coaches, I might be able to get a scholarship," I told her. "They sometimes hand them out on the spot."

"Well, you'd better get one," she replied. She wrote the check that very evening.

Two weeks later, I was on the field at the University of Pittsburgh's training facility with about three hundred other players. Pitt's practice field is built on the site of an old steel mill on the banks of the Monongahela River that was reclaimed about twenty years ago. A few homes are visible up on the hills through the thick trees, but the facility itself feels secluded and peaceful. Railroad tracks run parallel to the water, so you might see barges on one side of you and a train on the other—the only real reminders that you're actually smack-dab in the middle of a major city. Well, that and the signage for the Pittsburgh Steelers, with whom the school shares the buildings and fields. As a high school kid, I was awed by the fact that I was practicing on the same grass as the pros.

Maybe I was channeling some of the NFL grit that morning; each time the offense lined up, I would head straight for the quarterback, sacking player after player and breaking through every line they put in front of me. After one particularly good sack where I spun out and made it to the quarterback while the whistle still echoed, the

Pitt defensive line coach, Inoke Breckterfield, ran up and barked, "Come with me."

A little confused, I followed him as he walked off the field at a brisk pace. As soon as we got out of earshot of the other players, he turned to me with a huge smile and said, "I love what I see, and I want to give you a scholarship. I'm going to bring you to the head man's office right now."

His words didn't really sink in at first; the whole thing happened so suddenly. The next thing I knew, I was shaking hands with head coach Paul Chryst, who repeated Coach Breckterfield's offer: a full scholarship to the University of Pittsburgh, just like that. I sat in one of the empty chairs in front of Coach Chryst's desk while he explained: "The staff believes in you. We like what we see out there and Coach Breckterfield believes you can really play."

We chatted a little more about the program and what my goals were in school and with football, then Coach Chryst smiled and said I could get back out on the field. "Coach Joe Rudolph is our offensive coordinator. He can walk you back and answer any other questions you might have." Of course, they wanted me to commit on the spot, but I knew I needed to breathe for a second, call my family, and discuss things with my high school coaches to make sure everyone agreed this was the right move.

As we walked down the hallway, Coach Rudolph offered to let me use the phone in his office to call my family and let them know. "Give your mom a call," he suggested. "Get her on board."

I actually called my brothers first, because I thought they might better understand the significance of an on-the-spot offer, but not one of them picked up their phone. When I dialed Mom's number, she was exactly as excited as I was: "Really?!?! Oh my goodness, J! Unbelievable. I am so proud of you. Amazing. *Amazing!*"

About a week after I got home—a week spent thinking and praying and turning it over and over in my head—I told my mom I had made up my mind. She was thrilled, of course. Just before practice, I dialed up the Pitt office and spoke to Coach Rudolph: "I wanted to say thank you for the scholarship offer, and I will be committing to Pitt for the fall."

I felt about thirty pounds lighter with that decision off my shoulders. I had an offer, I had a plan, I had a clear path. All of the energy, encouragement, and resources my family had sunk into me had paid off; I had finally gotten my shot. But now I needed to make sure that shot counted for something. Now, the real work began.

I was navigating entirely new waters, treading the line between relief that I had an offer and fear that some small error on my part might cost me everything. Obviously, my performance on the field still mattered; I still needed to prove that I was worth Pitt's time, effort, and resources. That was where Rich's challenge to me when he gave me those custom cleats came into play. I rushed for 1,680 yards my senior year and racked up 150 carries. Even more important, though, I needed to make sure my ACT scores met Pitt's threshold, and I needed to get my grades up. While I was never in danger of being academically ineligible to play in high school, my GPA wasn't exactly stellar and my course load was not college-prep level. In preparation for my senior year that coming fall, I sat down with my coaches and pored over the course catalog and prerequisites I would need to be ready for college. I had no idea there was a specific set of classes I would need to take before even setting foot on campus.

As a result, we quickly realized I was going to require some extra tutoring to help raise my GPA and prepare me for the college board tests. I'm not going to lie, it was painful to see my other friends hop in their cars after school to go hang out while I had to ride a bus to a tutoring center in order to retake certain classes I'd blown off the first time around.

It seemed ironic that, on the one hand, I was on top of the world; players at other schools would tell me, "Congratulations on Pitt!" when we shook hands after each game. Yet here I was having to do some really basic and, frankly, *annoying* legwork just to be eligible to accept this amazing offer—things I really should have taken care of already. It was incredibly humbling, but it was also an experience for which I was strangely thankful. Even then, I recognized how significantly these lessons were shaping me into the kind of person I wanted to become. Looking back, I am the most grateful for the chance I had to reinvent myself to set me on a much more solid trajectory toward the kind of future I wanted.

Swallowing my pride and moving to another position to get playing time had proven to be the very move that had opened doors for me. If I hadn't been willing to adjust my attitude instead of clinging stubbornly to the one vision I had for myself as a player, I might never have had this chance. I also realized that no amount of ego was going to raise my GPA. It didn't matter how great I thought I was on the field; if I didn't do the work in the classroom, I would never get the chance to prove myself anywhere else. In fact, the more I was willing to sacrifice to raise my grades and prepare for the ACT—missed time with friends, my evening free time filled with extra classes, not being able to simply hang out and be one of the "cool seniors" after school—the more I realized that whatever dumb pride had been keeping me from raising my hand when I had a question in class was not worth whatever it was costing me in test points. Now if I didn't understand something, I asked about it. If I needed to go over a concept again, I stayed after class. My basketball coach, Mr. Kevin O'Connor, was also my English teacher, and he spent a lot of time tutoring me to become a better writer. It amazed me that my teachers were ready and willing to help—I had just never been willing to admit I needed the extra help and actually, you know, *ask for it.* When I weighed the option of having to admit I didn't understand a lesson versus having to turn down the scholarship because I hadn't achieved the minimum GPA, the choice became pretty clear. I could voluntarily humble myself now, or I could be forcefully humbled later. And when I saw my GPA rise from a 1.7 going into my senior year to a 2.5 at graduation and an ACT score that met Pitt's enrollment requirements, I knew it had all been worth it.

I left for Pitt's summer training camp in late June—the day after Sean's graduation party, in fact. Even as I met the teammates who were to become some of my closest friends over the next four years—Rachid, Des, Tony, Justin, Alex, Devon—one thought kept running through my head: "I want to do this *right*." Making team meetings on time, remembering appointments, paying my bills, giving my best at practice—I knew the only person responsible for me was *me*. When classes started, I knew I was the only person who would force myself to stay on top of my homework. I was the only person who could make the best choices about how I allocated my budget and how I used my time. The freedom was mine, and so were the consequences.

I watched Deion Sanders's Hall of Fame speech, where he described the decision he made as a freshman at Florida State that he was going to be great, and how that mindset early on put him on the right path. I went back to my dorm and turned that over in my head before I went out to the PNC Bank branch on campus and opened my first checking account. I held my debit card gingerly in my hand when it arrived; it was powerful to have total control over my own money, but it was a little scary, too. I didn't have a backup plan. If I messed things up by not doing my classwork or by getting myself into debt early on, I would blow my one shot. I kept that at the forefront of my mind, opting to stay in most nights to do pushups and study game tape instead of going out. My brothers were great about encouraging me. They called and texted me just to say, "You're so close to your dream. You're almost there! Just stay focused." So I tried to do exactly that.

When I looked around, I saw so many students who were enjoying their newfound freedom a lot more than I seemed to be, but I had to stay dedicated to bigger goals. I was away from home for the first time, too; in fact, I had never been more than two hours away from Erie my entire life. It would have been awesome to get to cut loose, but at what cost? I thought about everything my mom and brothers had sacrificed to get me there. I thought about the investment my coaches and teachers had made to prepare me for this chance. I thought about what the football staff at Pitt had risked by taking a chance on me. Was I really going to chance throwing away all of their hard work—and mine, for that matter—just because I felt I deserved to live larger than my current circumstances allowed?

As football practice got underway, I took a lot of pride in knowing that the coaches at Pitt must have had big plans for me based on how we had met. I couldn't wait to see what they had in store for me. Even though I had been recruited as a defensive lineman, my coaches quickly moved me over to running back when they saw my speed on the field, which was more than fine with me. I was determined to impress them on game day, but I had forgotten to factor in one little detail: I was a true freshman.

I played in almost every game in the 2013 season, but never as the starter, which was a heck of a blow after riding the bench throughout my junior year of high school. My previous season had been phenomenal; why weren't the coaches letting me show what I could do now?

Eventually, I realized I needed to ask myself a very basic question: Were the same coaches I believed to be insightful enough to offer me a full ride on the spot also brilliant enough to know how to best manage the talent on their roster? Either they knew what they were doing or they didn't, and I had to be willing to accept their leadership if I wanted to be part of the team. As hard as it was at times not to get upset that my name was not at the top of the depth chart (again), I had to be willing to continue to do the work so I could be ready when my time came.

The step back from the limelight forced me to look at the most successful players and determine what they were doing to set themselves apart. I was already giving my all in practice and in the weight room—I was completely committed to being the hardest worker—but if my status quo still wasn't enough to earn me the top spot, maybe there was something more I needed to learn to continue to refine myself. That's when I started to notice people's trays in the cafeteria. The guys who were starting and consistently making the biggest plays were the ones who had the healthiest foods on their plates. The more I looked for it, the more I saw a direct correlation in performance between the guy who had fries each night and the guy who opted instead for the steamed broccoli. I couldn't believe that I had been overlooking something so simple and fundamental— something I'd been taught since I was a kid. Surely the impact of diet couldn't be that dramatic, could it?

That's when it hit me: At the most elite levels, the differences don't have to be dramatic to stand out. Everyone playing at a Division I college is going to be good. It's the small differences and the seemingly minor choices that set apart the people who have talent from the people who can really impact the game. I'm not going to lie: It knocked me down a peg or two to realize that every guy there had been a stud at his high school, too. I knew I wasn't ever going to earn the starting spot on talent alone because *everyone* was talented. But I also realized that hard work wasn't enough, either. I had to be willing to shift my entire way of thinking and train myself in fundamentals like diet, drills, and discipline. The moment I was willing to not only accept that humbling reality but also take the steps to act on it, everything changed for me. In our final game of the 2013 season, I rushed for 229 yards, breaking the school's previous bowl game record, which NFL Hall of Famer Tony Dorsett had set back in 1976. I was named the game's MVP. I had been willing to break out of old habits and rebuild myself while I waited for my turn, and it paid off. Not only did I have an amazing end to my freshman season, that game became the catalyst for the following year.

Our season opener set the tone for my sophomore season. I racked up 14 carries for a total of 153 yards and four touchdowns in our 62–0 blowout against Delaware. Over the course of our thirteen games that season, I racked up 1,765 yards on 298 attempts, earning the seventh-highest ranking in college football and the top spot in our conference. I also scored 26 rushing touchdowns, which set a new ACC record. In fact, I broke three regular-season records at Pitt: most rushing touchdowns (24), most total touchdowns (24), and most overall points (144). What made it even sweeter was that all those records had been set by Tony Dorsett, one of my childhood heroes, back in 1976—the same year he won the Heisman Trophy. I also broke the conference single-season record for rushing touchdowns and total touchdowns set in 2009.

My mom and all my brothers made it to just about every game; Sean and Carson had press passes thanks to Sean's sportscaster dad, and they were able to travel every week—both home and away—to work cameras on the sidelines and cheer me on up close. (The two of them will neither confirm nor deny that they engaged in some pretty severe trash talk with an opposing player whom I knocked out of bounds on one of my three touchdown runs during our game against Duke.)

In each game, I kept finding holes on the field, breaking through tackles, and reaching the end zone. All the buzz toward the end of the season was that the ACC Player of the Year award was going to end up as a two-way race between me and Jameis Winston, the Florida State quarterback who was still making waves following his Heisman season. I know that I should probably say I didn't think about that and just concentrated on playing the game. The truth is, though, I really *did* hope I would win. Any true competitor should; there is nothing wrong with hoping that your hard work gets recognized. It only becomes a problem when you pin your sense of self-worth on whether or not you get certain accolades—and if you forget Who is ultimately behind your success.

That year was the kind of season every player dreams of, and it was happening to *me*. But as the season progressed and my numbers climbed, a strange thing started to happen—something I didn't even notice at first: I started praying less. Cockiness can take root in any number of ways; it doesn't have to be walking around announcing to everyone you meet, "I'm the best." It can be a quieter, more subtle change in your personality as you disconnect from the things that once kept you grounded. I felt on top of the world. Every run, every pass, every game seemed to fall in my favor. I was so convinced nothing bad could possibly happen to me that I stopped paying attention to the source of all of my accomplishments. It's not that I stopped believing in God, but I started ignoring His role in bringing so many incredible opportunities my way.

E. J. Borghetti, the media relations coordinator and assistant athletic director at Pitt, called me into his office half an hour before practice one afternoon in early December and slid a piece of paper across the desk to me—a printed email from the ACC governing body announcing that I had been voted the player of the year. He grinned broadly and so did I, but I also knew that my season would not have been any less impactful for myself or for my team even if I had not been given that honor.

As I thought about my upcoming junior season, I couldn't help but feel a huge rush of pride in what I had done and what the chatter would be about me next year as I eyed entering the NFL draft. I had already posted some pretty amazing numbers, and I had no intention of going anywhere but up.

But in all my ambitious plans, I began to put my faith in my own strength, my own talent, my own work ethic, my own discipline. As I neglected my prayer life, I started focusing on the idea that

I somehow had an unquestioned right to the success I was now enjoying. I had paid my dues and was now rushing past every obstacle in my path. My time to slow down, be patient, and wait my turn was behind me. In my mind, every victory I was enjoying was because I had *earned* it. No one would ever think of benching me now, right?

All these thoughts swirled in my head as I prepared for the 2015 season opener against Youngstown State.

How quickly things can change.

* * *

My whole life's journey has been about two essential qualities: staying patient and believing there are better days ahead. One of the biggest internal challenges we can face is finding the balance between knowing our worth, honoring our talent, and being humble enough to wait. It is easy to slide in one direction or the other: "I'm the best there is, and these coaches are fools if they can't see that" or "It's an honor just to be on the team, so I won't speak up." It's the middle position that's the hardest to maintain.

Looking back, I can see how those lessons in humility prepared me for the next chapter ahead—before I even knew what was next. The most striking moment was when I tore my MCL during that Youngstown season opener. After all the praise my sophomore season, I tried to keep my head on straight, but it became easy to think that I was invincible. I believed whatever I wanted to accomplish was possible, through *my* strength alone. As my stats started climbing, I began to lose sight of the real source of my strength and the many opportunities granted to me over the years.

I wanted all my hard work to pay off right away and my dreams to come true immediately. But as I learned both as an impatient running back in high school and as an impatient freshman in college, we shouldn't be in such a rush to succeed that we miss the opportunity to figure out how to best do that. Sometimes, those unwelcome pauses give us an opportunity to discover new aspects about ourselves that help us grow or allow us to uncover hidden talents. Life is rarely an all-or-nothing proposition; it's okay to defer the drive for success for a little while as you figure out the right plan. Now, I encourage younger athletes I meet not to try to live too soon—in other words, don't think you have to have it all immediately. Success can come by degrees—in fact, it *should* come to you that way rather than all at once so that you are prepared for it, able to appreciate it, and have enough perspective to make wise calls about where to go next. It's essential to experience seasons of humility in order to help you hone your skills, focus, and appreciate the chance when it finally comes along.

Even in the NFL, I found I needed to be humble enough to wait for my chance. My first season with the Steelers, I didn't see very much playing time starting behind Le'Veon Bell, one of the highest-ranking running backs in the entire league. It killed me to have finally made it to the NFL and still be stuck behind someone, but I knew I had to find my place on the team. Instead of allowing myself to become frustrated, I reflected on my previous experiences in high school and college, kept my head down, learned the ropes, studied Bell's playing style, and honed my own skills. Eventually, when I was ready, I knew I would have a chance to get out there and accomplish everything I hoped to for my team.

That chance came a lot sooner than I had anticipated when Bell sat out the 2018 season due to a contract dispute. Because I had been willing to watch and work the previous season, I was ready to step into the starting role when the team needed me. Within the span of a season, I went from 144 rushing yards and no touchdowns in 2017 to 973 rushing yards and 12 touchdowns in 2018. In fact, I ended the year tied for the third-most rushing touchdowns by a single player that season! As exciting as those numbers are, they didn't happen in a vacuum. They were the end result of years of hard work and invisible time spent in training and drilling in order to be ready when my shot came. Those numbers reflected the shared effort of my coaches, my teammates, my family, and everyone else who had poured themselves into my support, discipline, attention, and mentorship. It was a lot easier to stay humble when I considered my stats from that angle.

Ultimately, though, being willing to be humbled means that you are able to be realistic about where you are and what you need. It means putting in the effort to make something happen rather than expecting it to be handed to you, but it also means remembering that you are part of a much bigger story. Being humbled is not the same as being defeated; it's the opposite, in fact. When you are humbled, it means you have learned from the experience—that something in your character has shifted to make you a little more teachable.

Don't let your ego steer the ship. Don't fall into the trap of believing that your team's success—whether the team is your coworkers, your teammates, or even your family—rises or falls based on you alone. On the other hand, respect yourself enough to be your own advocate. Believe in your abilities, your strength, your skills, and your goals. You owe that to yourself. Being patient does not mean sitting still; it means not rushing an opportunity before the right time. It doesn't mean simply shutting down, either. Disciplined patience means getting *and staying* prepared—and it takes humility to admit that you have room to grow while you wait for your shot.

What I didn't yet understand heading into my junior year was that the same grit that never let me quit was also the same stubbornness that kept me from admitting when I was in pain or needed help. I didn't yet understand the difference between dedication and obsession. Rather than recognizing my talents as gifts that I should cultivate and celebrate, I started to see them as a birthright that made me untouchable by disappointment. God used my MCL tear to get my attention and force me to be honest about my limitations. It was that honesty that led to my eventual diagnosis of Hodgkin's lymphoma.

Don't let your strength cost you the battle. When we rely too much on our own strength, we forget that we are ultimately not in control. If we refuse to admit that God is stronger than we can ever be, we deny Him the chance to work in us, perform the miracles we ask of Him, and help us grow. But if we are willing to accept help and admit when the challenge is more than we can handle on our own, then and only then is there room for us to allow the strength of God and of others to aid us in our fight.

CHAPTER 3

TRUST THE PLAN

Plot twists. We love them in movies; we hate them in real life.

I know this is true because I have seen it firsthand.

Just below a three-inch scar on my right knee, I have a tattoo that reads "Jeremiah 29:11: 'For I know the plans I have for you,' declares the LORD, 'plans to prosper you and not to harm you, plans to give you hope and a future.'" When I'm uncertain about my circumstances, all it takes is one look at that tattoo to remind me not to give up or walk out before I can see God's plan at work in my life.

I want you to think about that verse for a minute. Really let it sink in. God, the Creator of the Universe, has a specific vision and direction for my life, and for yours as well. He already mapped out a plan for my life that is designed not to cause me harm but to encourage me and point me toward my destiny. That's a lot of really deliberate action and forethought on the part of our Creator. I've always believed that all the disjointed, disruptive, and disappointing events served some kind of larger purpose, but never has that belief been put to the test—and proven true—in a bigger way in my life than during the fall of 2015.

The three months following Pitt's season opener against Youngstown State were brutal. First there was the MCL injury itself, followed immediately by the news that I was out for the season. After receiving that news, the surgery and grueling rehab were no big deal by comparison. Nothing could have been more devastating to me than hearing that my football dreams were on hold or that my draft prospects had disappeared in a moment. No amount of physical pain could compare to what I was feeling inside. I was frustrated. I was angry. I was confused. And I was completely unprepared for what came next.

The second the doctors gave me the green light to start working out again after my MCL surgery—at the end of September, about three weeks after my injury—I hit the weight room. I wasn't going to be stupid about my training and put myself at risk for reinjury by overdoing it, but I was determined to produce the quickest comeback anyone had ever seen. I had lost some muscle mass while I was laid up, but I figured I could make that up in no time if I pushed myself just a little bit harder. My goal was to get back into peak shape before Christmas and be ready to play again in time for our spring game.

At first, it seemed like all was going according to plan. But soon there was a problem—a sneaking whisper in the back of my head

I tried to ignore, telling me something was wrong. I struggled to recover from runs that used to be no problem. When I tried to lift weights, I experienced an intense pressure in my head, like it was being squeezed in a vice. And then there were the night sweats. I would fight all night to fall asleep, only to wake up in the morning after less than an hour of rest, my bed soaked in sweat. None of this made any sense. I was an athlete. I ate right. I was physically healthy. But my body seemed to be failing me anyway. My symptoms stumped specialist after specialist until finally, out of sheer desperation, I made an appointment with an ear, nose, and throat doctor, thinking I might have a severe sinus infection that was causing my head pain.

Everything looked clear during the appointment: no ear infection, no sinus issues, nothing to indicate that anything was wrong. So much for that theory. But before I left her office, she told me she was going to send me for a chest X-ray, "Just in case." The answer to the question "Just in case *what*?" never even crossed my mind. I just went to the appointment and then headed home to try to squeeze in another workout before bed. The doctor's office called me a few hours later and told me I needed to see my regular physician, Dr. Robert Ferris, the next day for further tests.

First thing in the morning, I showed up at the clinic. The University of Pittsburgh Medical Center is huge, with several different massive buildings scattered around campus and downtown. It was strange to be walking into an enormous twelve-story building that was surprisingly quiet and still before it filled up with people for the day. I made my way to Dr. Ferris's office and checked in. They took me back right away. No one should ever get that many needle pricks or have that much blood drawn before their morning coffee. As the lab printer spit out the labels for all of the different vials, I was amazed at how long the paper was; I could have wrapped it around my neck and used it as a scarf. But all I really cared about was feeling better, so I didn't think much about it. I was just ready to have a diagnosis so I could get a treatment plan and recovery schedule—and get back to playing—as quickly as possible. When I was done at the lab, Dr. Ferris sat me down and explained that the X-rays had shown some suspicious masses in my chest. He was concerned it might be lymphoma.

I had never even heard of lymphoma, so his words hardly fazed me. I mean, I knew it couldn't be great news, but I didn't automatically realize that it was a type of cancer. Maybe that was a good thing because it kept me from freaking out right away. Since most of the pain seemed to be in my face and head, I still thought I had some kind of a bad cold; if we could just knock that out of my system, I'd be fine. But when Dr. Ferris told me he wanted to do a biopsy, something in my gut kept nudging me: *I have to tell Mom.*

She was worried enough about my knee; I didn't see the point in adding to her stress if it turned out that my head pain was really just something dumb like a sinus infection. But I couldn't quiet that nagging voice, so I reluctantly dialed the phone and told her everything. Unlike me, my mom instantly realized the implications of lymphoma.

Mom did a great job of keeping her fears under wraps, but I could still detect concern in her voice when she told me she was going to drive down that night and accompany me to the biopsy the next day. I'm glad she came. Once I started doing a little research on lymphoma, I realized that I was potentially facing something way bigger than anything I could have ever prepared for.

Unlike when I got the torn-MCL diagnosis, I didn't cry. I wasn't sad; I was angry and in shock. After everything I had already gone through, God was going to pile cancer on top of it, too? How was that consistent with the loving Father I'd always believed cared about me and my life? It wasn't fair to my mom, it wasn't fair to my family, it wasn't fair to my team, and it wasn't fair to *me*. What about *my* plans and *my* dreams? I lost what was supposed to be my best season, and now I was faced with the possibility that I might even lose my life. If this really did turn out to be cancer, couldn't God have let me at least keep football before dropping something like this on my lap?

As I turned that idea over (and over) in my head, I remembered something one of the doctors had told me: If I had continued playing in my distressed physical condition, with my white blood cell counts as elevated as they were and a tumor compressing the veins near my heart, there was a very good chance that I could have gone into cardiac arrest on the field. That could have been it for me. If I had a heart attack in the middle of a game, we would have had no idea what had caused it—possibly until it was too late to undergo any kind of treatment. The more I thought about that, the more my perspective shifted. Maybe God *had* to take football away in order to save my heart. He knew how stubborn I was about playing through pain, so He had to go to greater lengths to make sure I didn't get in the way of what He was doing. And if He went to such lengths to save my heart, would He then let me lose the battle to the disease?

Then it hit me: *This was exactly the way things were supposed to happen.*

Everything had to occur precisely as it did to bring me to where I was in that moment. Given the choice, I never would have allowed my MCL to be torn, but my injury was the very thing God used to grab my attention and get me off that football field. God used that torn MCL to save my life, but with my limited outlook, I would have done everything in my power to stop that tear from happening in the first place. And if I'd had any power to do so, I would've prevented all the other big things that God had in store for me.

That was the realization I carried with me into surgery, when they made a two-inch incision in my neck to slice out some lymph nodes for testing. That was the comfort I held on to during the stressful wait as I answered every unknown phone call with equal parts eagerness and dread. I wanted to know if it was cancer, but I didn't want to know that *I* had cancer. Just because I knew God had a plan didn't mean I wasn't afraid of what that plan might look like. Most of all, I clung to the hope that there was a reason for everything I was experiencing. This faith in what I couldn't see—couldn't observe with my human eyes—helped me keep the worst of the fear at bay.

Finally, on a cold morning the first week of December, we got a call that the results were in. Mom and I drove to the hospital. We didn't talk a whole lot. What was there to say at that point?

A few minutes after we arrived, I was called back to the exam room, my mom and my athletic trainer on my heels. The paper on the vinyl table crinkled as I sat on it, but otherwise the room was so quiet that I swore others could hear my nervous heartbeat. Even though I tried to keep my concerns to myself to save my mom the worry, I felt so much calmer just knowing she was next to me at that moment. The door opened, and Dr. Ferris squeezed in with a very serious look on his face. He pulled my file up on the computer. As he started talking about what the various tests showed, his voice faded into the background while my eyes slid to one line of text at the bottom of the screen: "Symptoms compatible with lymphoma."

There it was. Any hope for a different diagnosis evaporated. I could only vaguely hear the sound of Dr. Ferris's voice explaining the procedure the pathologists had used in examining the biopsy results.

Unable to contain my anxiety any longer, I cut Dr. Ferris off mid-sentence. "The last line says . . ."

Dr. Ferris gently confirmed what I'd read as my mom burst into tears. I was filled with an incredible feeling of defiance. I didn't care about the odds. It didn't matter to me if the survival rate was 85 percent or 5 percent, I was going to beat this thing. I couldn't imagine that God would bring me this far just to let me go now. If I was going to trust the plan—really, truly trust it beyond all reason or logic—I couldn't even entertain the option that there was any other outcome for me than complete recovery.

I would be lying if I told you that I was totally at peace with the news; I wasn't. I was angry all over again at how unfair everything seemed. I was frustrated that I was further than ever from my dream of getting back out on the field. A lot of the calm I had felt previously evaporated, even though I was glad that my injury had led to my diagnosis. I knew there was a bigger plan at work, but I couldn't feel grateful for the fight I'd been handed.

I still had no idea just how big the plan really was.

As soon as the news of my diagnosis went public, the fan support started pouring in. It was an incredible feeling to know my community was rallying behind me and that football fans across the country were praying for me. But I only really began to understand how much meaning there was in my struggle when I started receiving letters and social media messages from other cancer patients. I heard from people who had no connection to western Pennsylvania and no interest in college football. There were first graders going through cancer treatments of their own who wrote to me, excited to talk to someone else who knew what they were enduring. I got messages from sixty-year-olds who'd survived their battles with Hodgkin's and told me about all the things I had to look forward to on the other side of this fight—getting married, having kids, accomplishing all the dreams I had for myself. The struggle would be miserable, they assured me, but it would also be very, very worth it.

I used to believe that the ultimate point of my life was to be a football player. Ever since I was in kindergarten, I knew I wanted to be a professional athlete when I grew up. There was never anything else—no backup, no "plan B." And while I'm incredibly blessed to have had that dream work out for me, I now see that I get to be so much more than just a football player. This story was never about *me*, but, rather, the ways in which I would use the platform God gave me to share His message and encourage other people. Football has allowed me to share my story with more people than would have otherwise been possible, but football does not *define* me. Only God can do that.

Maybe you've experienced a plot twist in your life or come to a crossroads, too. Perhaps you've just been knocked flat by a career setback, a financial upheaval, the ending of a relationship, a death, or a medical event. These things happen to all of us. Life serves us up something we aren't expecting, haven't prepared for, and didn't want. When that happens, you really only have two choices. You can either face your fears, or you can give in to them. And I can tell you from experience, it's a lot easier to face your fears when you believe there's a purpose behind what you're experiencing. What you are going through right now is *not* the whole story—it's just one chapter along the way. There is a point to your pain. There is meaning behind your struggles. And what great story have you ever heard where there isn't conflict? Struggle means that God is setting you up for something better—something significant. Trust that even when you can't see to the end of whatever road you're on, there is something bigger at work.

Every day, I am amazed that my experiences could encourage someone on the other side of the country—or even the planet!—to keep fighting their personal fight. My cancer was nothing I would've ever chosen to be part of my story, but that's because my own vision for my life was way too small. My plan was about having a job and making a name for myself; God's plan was about having a purpose. Never in a million years would I have imagined that He could use me to give hope to others. I didn't do anything special; I simply didn't give up the belief that there was, in fact, a master plan.

If we give up on the plan because it's not going our way, if we walk out on the story because we don't like the sudden curveball we've been tossed, if we throw up our hands when our situation seems hopeless, we will never get to experience the greater reality God has in store for us. When we trust that the plan has been put together for our benefit, fear evaporates. When we live from a place of trust instead of fear, we become capable of living a life of true significance.

CHAPTER 4

LEAD FROM WHERE YOU ARE

I was beat. Every muscle ached. I couldn't imagine I had an ounce of water left in my body after what I had just sweated out as I wobbled on unsteady legs toward the tunnel.

The University of Pittsburgh shares Heinz Field with the Pittsburgh Steelers, and as I stumbled toward our locker room, I couldn't help but steal a glance over toward the Steelers' side of the facilities. It was my breakout sophomore season, and I had just pushed myself in practice even harder than I had when I was still fighting for a starting spot. There were definitely times when I wanted to slack off a bit. There were moments when I felt like my performance in the prior week's game had earned me the right to go a little bit easier in the weight room or running drills. But I also knew that if I did, I would be sending a message to my teammates that I thought I was somehow better than them—as if the rules didn't apply to me because I was having a good season and therefore deserved special treatment. Because of that, I pushed myself even harder, so no one could say I thought I was above putting in the hard work. Every day I tried to outdo whatever I had done the day before. As I write this, almost five years later, I can still taste the sweat in the corners of my mouth and feel the pounding in my temples that afternoon as I pushed my body toward the showers.

"I hope this is all worth it," I mumbled.

Even as I carried that sense of extra responsibility in college, knowing the hopes my family had for me and the sacrifices they had made, I also found a tremendous freedom in the fact that I'd never really had a chance to lead before. Years after my brothers graduated from high school, I was still "the youngest Conner boy" at McDowell High School and around Erie. Starting at Pitt was my first chance to carve out an identity on my own terms, and I knew from day one what I wanted that identity to be.

There was an unspoken but natural seating arrangement in our team meetings: freshman in the back, sophomores ahead of them, juniors in the middle, seniors at the front, and the team captains in the very first row. In the first few meetings of my college career, as I sat with my back against the wall in the final row and watched everyone file in, I made a promise to myself. I was going to get down to the front of the room as quickly as I could. Obviously, I'd move a few rows forward each year, but that wasn't what I was thinking of.

I wanted to be in a captain's seat; those spots were filled by players the coaches believed had enough talent to be visible *and* had the right character to lead. The very front of the room wasn't reserved for the players with the best stats. It wasn't for the ones who ran their mouths or beat their chests or demanded that people recognize how great they are. The guys who sat down in the captains' spots just carried themselves differently. It wasn't an arrogant swagger; it was a straight-shouldered, upright confidence that didn't demand respect from their teammates, but revealed that they already had it.

That was the kind of man I wanted to be. My ambition wasn't to become captain—it was to become the kind of person who had the character to be named captain. The distinction may seem small, but it's significant. Seeking the title wasn't about the honor and the power; it was about growing into a person qualified to be considered for the role.

For me, leadership has always been a behind-the-scenes thing. I've never been someone who makes locker room speeches, probably because I'm not a particularly talkative person. Even in high school, I let other people make the dramatic pregame pep talks. I guess every team needs a leader who can do that, but I'm just not that guy. That being said, I turn into a motivation machine on the sidelines. Coach Soboleski used to ask how I could be so quiet ahead of the game and then outdo the cheerleaders during it. I guess I don't see myself as someone who *gets* people pumped up—but I will cheer my face off to *keep* them pumped up. I also didn't engage in a lot of trash talk during games. I had watched enough of my brothers' games over the years to know that jawing off at someone usually just led to a fight breaking out. I made it my goal to get people on their feet on the sidelines and calm them down on the field. I don't know that I made a conscious decision to do this, but my high school coaches all recalled that if I saw a teammate about to get in a fight with a player on the other team, I would be the first one to put my hands on his shoulders and try to talk him down before the refs got involved. I value peace over drama, and I guess providing that calming presence was just something I did instinctively to help bring it about. I wanted my teammates to know I was there with them and that I trusted them to be able to take a breath and make the right choice in a heated situation.

The best leaders, from my perspective, are not the people who stand in front of a group, facing them. That's the coach's job. A true leader is someone who is facing the same direction as everyone else, leading the charge on the field with them. A true leader is right in the thick of things with everyone else. That's why I resolved early on that I wasn't ever going to try to elbow my way to the front of the group. I was just going to work harder, exactly where I was, in order to become a better athlete and teammate. I never learned much about how to improve my speed or build my strength from speechmakers anyway; I'd rather concentrate on developing my skills. If, in the process, someone decided that what I was doing was worth watching or imitating—great! That meant my effort was probably translating to a better performance on the field or out in everyday life. People generally avoid copying what fails, after all. If what I was doing helped inspire someone else to up their game, too, that meant I was making the best contribution I could to my team. I would rather be just one of the crowd on a successful team than a standout on a failing team. When one person improves, their team gets that much better, too. It's simple, but it's the kind of impact I wanted to have.

I carried this leadership philosophy with me to college as I quickly realized that I was probably not going to be a major influencer on the team as a true freshman. The best thing I could do for my team was simply to prepare to be the strongest possible player for whenever my time came, so that became my goal. I worked hard to make sure I was staying on top of my classes to keep my GPA where it needed to be. I gave 100 percent at every practice, workout, meeting, and game. I made small changes that had the potential for major impact, like becoming much more health-conscious about my diet. Basically, I committed myself to being the best I could be, exactly where I was.

It worked. I didn't just catch the notice of my coaches, who began to reward the improvements that came from those efforts with more playing time; I also won the respect of my teammates, who knew I was a guy they could always rely on to know the playbook and be ready to execute it. By committing myself to being the best person *and* the best player I could be, I was communicating to the people around me that I was worthy of their trust. Whatever personal success I enjoyed on the field, I was still going to put the team first. And trust, as everyone knows, is at the heart of any healthy team.

I was grateful for the fantastic examples of leadership I had on our coaching staff at Pitt, including the interim strength-and-conditioning coach, and as my sophomore year started to ramp up, I found myself increasingly encouraged and inspired by him. Kenechi Udeze had gone to USC and been a first-round draft pick of the Vikings. Everything seemed to be going great with his career until he was diagnosed with lymphoma after four years in the pros and was given only a 17 percent chance to live. He underwent radiation therapy and a bone marrow transplant with a donation from his brother, who happened to be a match; now, he was working at Pitt for a year. I thought the world of Coach Udeze. He was one of those people who just exuded motivation, which made us all want to work harder as a result.

"The game can be taken from any one of you at any minute," Coach Udeze would remind us. "You have to appreciate each chance you've got to play and give it your all every day." I used to spend a lot of time in his office, trying to absorb more of his drive and wisdom. He represented to me exactly what leadership should be: embracing the role you are in right now and doing the absolute best at it that you can. Of course, Coach Udeze would have liked a longer professional career, but instead of becoming bitter over what his cancer had taken from him, he embraced his role as someone who could positively influence the next generation of players. At the time, I considered him a great mentor that God had put in my life to help me learn from during my breakout season, but I had no idea how much more significant his mentorship would prove to me as I moved into my own health crisis.

We had a new head coach my junior year, as Coach Chryst left to take the top spot at Wisconsin. Pat Narduzzi, the defensive coordinator at Michigan State, was offered the head position at Pitt. As sorry as I was to see Coach Chryst go, I was also very hopeful about the new head coach coming in. Other than Pitt, Michigan State was the main school that had been especially interested in me when I was in high school, and a big part of my interest in *them* was because of Coach Narduzzi and the great reputation he had as a leader. He was a no-nonsense coach who didn't utilize gimmicks or flashy tricks to build excitement. His approach was more old-school—inspiring confidence in his players by pushing us beyond our own limits. It was exhausting work, but it was also incredibly rewarding and helped me draw the best out of myself.

When I tore my MCL in the season opener, I made sure that my team knew I wasn't going anywhere. "I greatly appreciate everyone's support and well-wishes," I said in an official statement released by the school. "This is a temporary setback, and I'm going to work even harder to bounce back. Even though I won't be able to play this season, I'm going to be right beside my teammates and help them in every way I can to have a great season." That was the most important message I wanted to get out there: just because I wasn't on the field didn't mean I wasn't still going to train and plan and fight right alongside everyone else.

I continued to attend every practice and every meeting. I was there for every home game and traveled for each away game because I wanted to be the kind of leader my teammates and coaches could trust. Even though my physical situation had changed, they knew I wouldn't shirk my team responsibilities. Because I had just come off such a dominant season, I naturally took on more of a leadership role, but I also understood the importance of developing my character so that I wasn't just about big plays on game day, but also the behavior the coaches wanted from us *leading up* to game day.

It felt like my dreams had been crushed when I blew out my knee—but I also knew it was only temporary. I was determined to overcome the pain and disappointment and get back out there with my team as quickly as possible. As much as I hated the fact that I was sidelined for the rest of the season, I was convinced that if I could just push myself hard enough, I'd be able to fight back better and stronger than my doctors and trainers imagined. That's what a leader is supposed to do, right? Try to keep things under control to bring about the best possible outcome. I had a responsibility I did not take lightly. I was going to give it my all.

In fact, my commitment to lead by example became even more significant after my injury. I no longer had game stats to back me up. Now, I had to model attitude and commitment to the game through every means *except* making big plays. I had to walk the walk rather than just run the ball.

With that in mind, I didn't just show up for physical therapy; I hit it like it was the NFL scouting combine. I wanted to do extra reps, higher tension on the machines, heavier weights. To me, this wasn't just about healing—it was about conquering the injury and reasserting control over my body. But that illusion of control was completely destroyed as I sat in a small exam room, listening to the doctor outlining my biopsy results and staring at the words "symptoms consistent with lymphoma" on the computer screen. Literally nothing in my power could have prevented the cancer from forming. There was nothing I did to spark the cancer cells' rapid multiplication, and nothing I could have done to have stopped it. Everything about the situation was out of my control.

Now what? I thought to myself on the drive home from the hospital after hearing my lymphoma diagnosis. I knew I had to tell the team. My trainer, Rob Blanc, knew since he had gone to the appointment with me, but he said he wouldn't share the news with anyone until I had a chance to digest it a bit more and talk it over with my coaches. I really appreciated the fact that he understood that as important as it was for my team to be aware of the situation, it was still my news to share.

The team was preparing for our big game against Maryland, and the last thing I wanted to do was pull focus and cause a distraction.

Did I want to unburden myself by sharing this news? Absolutely. Was I hoping for a little reassurance and support from my teammates? Definitely. But I knew that I couldn't make this about me. The good of the team and the goals we shared had to come first.

I went back to the house I was sharing with a couple of guys, and I sat down in the living room, trying to figure out what I wanted to say. My teammate and roommate Rachid Ibrahim came walking in with a big bag of Chipotle for dinner. He dropped the bag on the counter and started rummaging for napkins, then he looked up and saw me sitting quietly on the sofa.

"Hey, man—how are you doing?" he asked.

Rachid was another running back who was also out for the season due to an injury, so I knew he could appreciate the frustration I was already facing because of my torn MCL. I also knew that I had better get used to saying the words, so I just looked at him and replied, "Bro, the doctor told me I have cancer."

Pause.

"You serious?"

I nodded.

Another pause.

He glanced at his burrito bowl and shook his head. "I—I can't even eat right now, man."

"I'm telling Coach tomorrow."

"I'm praying for you, James."

We spent the rest of the evening in silence.

It was a relief to have told someone without getting emotional. I just hoped I could manage the same thing the next day.

Ahead of our team meeting the next morning, I stopped by Coach Narduzzi's office and asked if I could talk with him. I explained the situation to him in plain terms, and he asked what he could do to support me in the months to come. Then he shared that his father had died from lymphoma, so the disease was one he especially hated. "Whatever you need," he assured me, "we are here for you."

We decided to book a team meeting and press conference for a few days later so I could share the news with everyone else. We figured people would assume I was going to make an announcement regarding my knee and whether or not I intended to come back and play again, but it was so much bigger.

As the team assembled, I got a little choked up seeing the freshmen file into the back row, right where I had been sitting just two years earlier, dreaming of how great it would be when I earned my seat up front. Needless to say, this wasn't the way I had imagined things would go.

Once everyone was seated, we dimmed the lights and a video about Eric Berry started to play on the big screen. Berry was a safety for the Kansas City Chiefs who had been diagnosed with Hodgkin's lymphoma and fought back successfully. It was an emotional piece, but I could tell that some guys were scratching their heads as to why Coach would've shown it. Was it to illustrate the body's power to heal itself, just like I was trying to heal from my MCL tear? Was it intended to say, "I have to remember that things could be worse than a knee injury"? As the lights came back up, Coach Narduzzi turned to me and said, "James, do you want to come up front for a minute?"

I stood in front of my team, took a deep breath, and forced myself into that part of the leadership role I generally tried to avoid: I gave a speech.

"I'll bet a lot of you are wondering why I showed you that video," I began. A number of heads nodded. "I have been given the same diagnosis. I have Hodgkin's lymphoma."

Looking out at the room, I saw six of my teammates drop their heads on their desks and a couple of others gasped.

Keep going, I willed myself silently. *Just get through this without crying and you'll be okay.*

I'd wanted to deliver that message calmly and confidently, but I stuttered as the words came out and I started tearing up. *No!* I thought angrily. *You are not going to make a big production out of this. You are a leader and it's your job to be strong, not to show weakness.* But I couldn't make my voice obey, and I could feel my cheeks start to get wet.

Suddenly, through my blurry vision, I saw the desks start to empty as everyone stood up to circle around me. All of these big, tough athletes were crying and hugging. They locked arms with me, and one of my teammates, Dennis Briggs, led a prayer. It was one of the most incredible moments of my life. Here, in this moment when I stood up alone to face everyone with difficult news, I was completely and immediately surrounded with love. After the prayer, the guys lined up and hugged me, one by one. Several of them thanked me for sharing as openly as I had. That confused me at first until I realized that my vulnerability had allowed my teammates to show their emotions, too. What I first thought was a moment of failure turned out to be a moment of authenticity that brought us closer as a team.

A few hours later, as I stepped out to face the cameras and publicly share my diagnosis, I felt more at peace because of the love and support I had just received from my teammates.

We rarely get to choose the exact circumstances in which we will be called upon to lead. We can lead quietly from within the team, through our actions and our choices. On the other hand, we may get called to lead from the front in a more individual role. Whatever the case, we all have a sense of what we are trying to accomplish by the way we conduct ourselves in those situations.

As leaders, or potential leaders, we probably have a general sense of things—of the dynamics and culture of the team and our vision for the direction in which we'd like to take our organization. But there is no guarantee that things will go according to our plans. What do we do then? How do we adapt when we can't be the leader we envisioned being?

When I emerged as a team leader at Pitt, I took that honor and responsibility seriously. I was committed to supporting and encouraging my fellow players through every circumstance I imagined we might possibly face in a season. And then the unimaginable happened. What do you do when the world's biggest monkey wrench is hurled into the middle of all your best intentions?

In situations like that, the only thing you can do is lead from where you are, not from where you wish you were. People will trust a leader who is genuine, and trust is the key to all effective leadership. Trust—real trust—is stronger than fear and can allow your team to move forward united in their purpose rather than separated by their worries.

Even though I could no longer be the first guy off the blocks during running drills or the last guy off the field at the end of practice, it didn't mean I couldn't still be the hardest working guy on the bench. Just because I wasn't able to make an impact on the field didn't mean I couldn't still make an impact on my teammates. I could still show up. I could still run drills. I could still attend team meetings and study the playbook and watch tape and keep my grades up. When I first set the goal of becoming a team leader, it was about cultivating the right habits and attitudes in myself instead of seeking to be a star. As I matured over the next two years, I came to appreciate my coaches' wisdom in selecting captains based on mindset and not the number of touchdowns or tackles a player made. I couldn't play, but I could still lead. My cancer couldn't touch my character.

During all of those long practices and trips with the team— every bit as painful emotionally as they were physically for me—I continued to be present for my team. I wanted to lead from where I was, even if it was not where I wanted to be. As I watched my reps in the weight room go down instead of up, I never allowed the discouragement to distract me from my goal of a full recovery. I just kept showing up, doing the work, encouraging the team, and doing my best to contribute to our shared goal however I could despite the setbacks, disappointments, and frustrations.

My dream of becoming captain came true the following season. I had managed to grow into the kind of person I wanted to be, the type of person my coaches believed was deserving of this position. That meant that for everything I had been doing right on the field, I had been doing just as much right off it.

During one of the last team meetings of the season, Coach Narduzzi stood in front of the room and announced, "Our captain rings came in today." He held the small blue boxes in his left hand and called us up while the team applauded and Coach gave us handshakes. That moment was profoundly bittersweet for me. I hadn't won a championship other than my fifth-grade basketball tournament, so I had never earned a ring before—and here was one that represented the hardest couple of seasons of my life. But as I returned to my seat, turned that ring around in my hand, and watched the light reflect off the diamonds, I was struck by the metaphor: diamonds are formed when carbon is put under immense pressure. That was a pretty apt summary of my journey. It also reminded me of the heart of true leadership: it's not about grabbing the headlines in the big wins, but about being in the thick of things with everyone else and inspiring them to keep moving forward. I absolutely loved the honor of having been selected, but I also realized that I didn't need to have the title of "Captain" to be a leader; I could lead right from where I was.

Leadership is about the choices you make much more than it will ever be about the wins you rack up. The beauty of leading from where you are is that anyone can do it, whether or not they've been given an official title. It's about how you show up, how you meet your commitments, and how you carry yourself through life.

All that time my junior season, when I thought I was just a few PT sessions away from a full recovery, my body was actually fighting a battle of which I was completely oblivious—a battle that was taking me even farther from where I felt I owed it to my team to be. But while I learned how to lead from where I was, no matter how far off course it felt, I also learned how to face one of the most difficult challenges of my life: fighting my cancer head-on to get my dreams back on track.

CHAPTER 5

FEAR IS A CHOICE

The human body is an incredible thing. It's the most complex machine ever designed, capable of both self-destruction and fierce self-preservation. Sometimes both are raging at the same time without a person even knowing it. When I watch game film, whether it's from a college game from five years ago or last week's matchup, I'm always a little amazed at what my body is capable of. I can't believe I was fighting for my life, completely unaware, for who knows how long—probably at least a year—before we even knew anything was wrong. And the human brain is even more incredible. The way it can frame and reframe experiences, the way it responds to devastation as well as victory—that three-pound organ can create walls and then propel a two-hundred-pound body past them. I know this because I was pushed beyond my limit every day, beyond any amount of pain, fatigue, nausea, and discouragement I could imagine. What I learned is that the human body really is an incredible thing, that we will all encounter obstacles bigger than we feel prepared to face—and that fear is a choice.

We don't get to choose if we will face frightening obstacles in life—at some point, we all have to confront things that scare us—but we do have control over what power fear has in our lives. As I stared down my own mortality at age twenty, it would have been easy to give in to my fears, but I quickly realized that giving these anxieties space in my head allowed them power over me.

Ignorance is bliss, as the saying goes, and I'll admit that I didn't know enough to be scared at first. I didn't even realize the implications of lymphoma until I called my mom and admitted that I was getting some tests done. There was a long pause on the phone as soon as I said the word; that was the moment it hit me that there may be more to that potential diagnosis than I realized. I called Michael, too, and his reaction was the same as Mom's.

Mom drove down to be with me for the biopsy, then we went home together to Erie, but I didn't tell anyone about the situation—not even Glen and Rich. I don't go in for drama or big gestures or huge emotional swings; I'd rather be even-keeled, steady, and understated. It never seemed worth it to me to get worked up over something I couldn't change. As I awaited word from my doctors, my brain struggled with the disparity between the enormity of what I might be facing and the subtlety of my emotions. Why make myself—or anyone else—have to deal with something if it ended up being nothing?

The Gallaghers invited me to go to the movies with them while I was in town, and we all sat in the back row of the Erie Tinseltown theater, taking up just about every seat. Like any red-blooded American, I was raised on the *Rocky* movies, so I was excited to see *Creed* and looking forward to taking my mind off of my health situation for two hours. The lights dimmed and the film started, showing Rocky coaching a young boxer. But then (SPOILER ALERT) there was a twist: It turns out the great Rocky Balboa is in for the ultimate fight of his life when he is diagnosed with lymphoma.

Seriously?

I couldn't help but laugh a little in disbelief. Here I was, trying to give my brain a break from all the cancer talk, and now I was watching my worst fears played out in front of me on a thirty-foot screen. Since I hadn't told Sean yet, I couldn't even share the absurdity of the moment with him. I just had to sit there and pretend like I was being entertained along with everyone else in the theater. But in that moment, it occurred to me that I had a choice about how I would respond to my immediate situation, just as I had a choice about how I would respond to the scene in the movie. I could view it as God picking on me and making me feel isolated, or I could see it as God saying, "You are not alone in your diagnosis, and you are not going to be alone in your fight."

Something shifted inside me between watching *Creed* and learning for sure I had lymphoma. While the cancer diagnosis was confirmed, I had come to a realization: fear is only what you make of it. The longer I sat with the idea of cancer and turned it over in my mind from every imaginable angle, the more power I felt I had. Those couple of days were like giving a good bleach scrub to the worries in my head as the looming threat of cancer started to diminish in my mind and my faith began to take off. I asked myself a pretty fundamental question: If God had already been acting so deliberately behind the scenes to protect me by taking me off the field until we found the tumor, why would I let fear take the front seat? Either I trusted Him to be on my side or I didn't. If He chose to heal me completely, then I would celebrate that. If He chose not to, then I had to believe there was a bigger reason. Faith could help me in this season of life. Why, then, would I choose to allow fear to control my emotions when it could actually do so little to help me?

I decided that I would not give fear a foothold or even entertain it as an option. Instead, I would choose a response to the diagnosis that would serve me infinitely better than fear ever could: patience.

I know that patience might not seem like the most obvious decision to make. Courage, strength, self-care—those are probably all a more typical response. And don't get me wrong—those things absolutely matter. But patience was actually the only choice left for me. I had been in such a rush to get through my junior season, to start working in the off-season, to make it to the draft, to get to the NFL and, now, literally none of that was going to happen on my timeline. At first, I was filled with panic about this disruption to all my plans. In my mind, I had to make everything happen *now* or else the life I had mapped out for myself was going to absolutely fall apart. But suddenly, all I could do was wait, and trust that there was a plan taking shape on the other side of this obstacle. My job was just to get through it, continuing to live and work toward my goals, but also accepting that I cannot control what will happen. I could be afraid during this period of uncertainty, but it would be a whole lot less difficult if I resolved instead to be patient.

I felt fear, and I chose to act with patience; I had to separate my reaction from my response. It's easy to confuse emotions and behaviors. It is true that we generally can't control what we feel—joy, sadness, nervousness, fear, etc. But we can control how we act on those feelings—courage, misery, resolution, or patience. Of course I felt scared and angry initially; I think anyone would. But after I sat with that fear for a little while, I realized that *my response to it* would be the only thing that either fed it or eradicated it. If I allowed my emotions to steer my behavior, I would be handing over what little power and control I had left.

I kept all of this at the forefront of my mind as I prepared to face the media for the press conference on December 4, 2015. I walked into the press room with my coaches, my family, and my doctors and took a deep breath.

> *Every day people are asking me if I'm going to the NFL or coming back to Pitt. I've got the answer today, and actually I will be back at the University of Pittsburgh. But when I take the field with my teammates again and run out of that tunnel is going to be up to God, because I got the unfortunate news just a few days ago that I've actually been diagnosed with Hodgkin's lymphoma . . .*
>
> *When I heard I've got cancer, I was a little scared. But fear is a choice. I choose to not fear cancer. I choose to fight it, and we're going to beat this thing. . . . I know God would never bring me to something He can't bring me through.*

Fresh from my emotional announcement to my team, I was proud of myself for maintaining my composure as I made that formal announcement. I also released a written statement to the media, in which I noted:

One year ago today I was asking myself, "Why me?" Why was I the lucky one to be getting the ACC Player of the Year award when I had so many teammates who deserved it as much as me? Now one year later, instead of asking, "Why me?" I am saying, "Why not me?" I can beat cancer.

I know there are so many people in the world who were told by their doctors this week that they also have cancer. I want them to know that together we can—and will—beat cancer.

I will play football again. I will be at Heinz Field again. I have the best coaches and teammates in the country. I thank God I chose Pitt because now I also have the best doctors in the country and together we will win. I know this city has my back.

Three days later, I sat in the waiting room of the Hillman Cancer Center, part of the University of Pittsburgh Medical Center, waiting to be called back for my first chemotherapy treatment. In an effort to stick with my resolution of not giving in to fear, I decided not to psyche myself out by reading up on what the experience was like. I was going to fight my cancer with everything I had. I was all in—whatever it took. I decided I'd rather go in with a clear head and zero expectations than build up an idea in my head and then be stressed when things didn't go exactly as I had anticipated them. This was a major step for me in choosing patience; I'm a planner. I inherited my love of to-do lists from my mom. I like to know exactly what is going to happen and when, but I recognized that this was an entirely new scenario for me. I had absolutely no control over what was going to happen, and I had to let go and accept that fact.

I was just grateful I didn't have to walk into that first treatment alone. I squeezed my mom's hand and shot a little "here-we-go" raised eyebrows look at Sean when the nurse called my name. What followed became a biweekly ritual of blood draws and wait time. As it turns out, there is no "chemo pantry" where the doctors just find the prepackaged treatment for your cancer and pull it down from the shelf, ready to go. Before every appointment, patients have a panel of labs drawn so the oncologists, phlebologists, hematologists, and whatever other "-ologists" are involved can analyze the results and concoct a unique formula based on an individual's blood counts. Knowing that every treatment is based on each person's individual needs and that such a brilliant team of men and women were hard at work with the singular goal of *saving my life* went a long way toward assuaging some of my fears.

Unfortunately, in my attempt to keep myself from getting too wrapped up in the details about what was coming, I left myself a little too much in the dark. It wasn't until I was seated in the large, soft chair in the treatment room and was shaking the hand of my nurse, Sarah, that I realized I had not even bothered to ask *how* the chemo would be administered. Was it a pill? A shot? A laser?

"You'll get an IV drip," Sarah explained as she put the numbing cream on my chest before inserting the three-inch port catheter. "Your job is to stay in this chair while the bag drains—you'll have two bags that take about forty-five minutes to an hour each to empty. I'll come in when it's time to hook up the next bag and we will monitor how you're doing."

Oh. No lasers. Well, that's not as cool, but it also doesn't sound too bad. I can handle an IV. I sat back in the chair, chatting a little with my mom and Sean, who had been admitted into the treatment room to keep me company. *Fear is a choice*, I reminded myself as we waited for Sarah to return and start the treatment. *I made the choice not to give it a foothold.*

Five minutes passed, then ten minutes. I thought Sarah was just going to grab the IV bags and would be right back, but clearly something was holding her up. Finally, the door opened and instead of seeing the pretty nurse with pale skin and dark hair, in walked a figure dressed like some kind of astronaut or nuclear waste disposal robot carrying a huge bag of glowing red liquid that looked like a feeder for zombie hummingbirds. "Here you go," came a muffled voice from behind the mask.

"Um . . . Sarah?" I said. "What's with the getup?"

"Chemotherapy medication is a very potent mix," she explained. "I have to wear safety gear while I handle it, so it doesn't get on my skin."

Oh. So not even a little drop can touch your skin, but two bags of that atomic lava are going into *my body? Cool, cool.*

Moving as carefully as a bomb specialist in a blast suit—and looking an awful lot like one, too—Sarah lifted the red bag with her arms gloved up to the elbows and hooked up the drip. "There you go," she said as the evil-looking stuff started to flow into my chest. "You can call me if you need anything."

My mouth managed to form the words "thank you" as she left, but my head kept repeating *fear is a choice, fear is a choice, fear is a choice*, in an effort to convince myself the words were true.

As I slowly got used to the strange sensation of liquid flowing into my body, I found I could breathe more easily and even make conversation as if this were any other day. Now that I knew what to expect, I could let go of any lingering fear. Fear, after all, is really just concern about the unknown. When you're a kid, it's not the monster itself hiding under your bed that is scary—it's wondering if he is going to reach out and grab you if you put your feet down. I mean, the monster might actually turn out to be friendly if you could sit down and talk together. It's not knowing what he might do that is at the root of your fear, not the monster itself.

Fear and faith had been battling each other in my head for the past few weeks, but I decided to let go of the worries that feed fear. I'd never know the future, but I could choose to arm myself in the present with a basic sense of preparation.

As I settled into the chemo chair, I realized that knowledge is the first step in overcoming fear. When you educate yourself about what you are facing, you eliminate some of the unknowns, which causes fear to lose a lot of its power. Now that I had a better idea of what I could expect each week, I didn't have to worry about what I didn't know. In my mind, I had equated preparation with control. Whenever I prepared in practice, I was taking control over my readiness on game day. When I made the decision not to research my treatment, I thought I was surrendering control, but all I was really doing was trying to walk forward in the dark.

Realizing that led me to the next step in overcoming fear: letting go of the things you can't control.

Anxiety arises from a sense of powerlessness over the things we can't influence, which leads to fear; we feel too small, too weak, or too inadequate to withstand our circumstances. But when I reminded myself that God was in control, I found I didn't need to stress myself out about all the little things that I couldn't manage on my own. It's that same stupid under-the-bed monster all over again. When you are afraid that it might reach out and grab your feet, you feel a tremendous sense of relief when your mom or dad comes in and snuggles with you until you fall asleep. They didn't make the monster go away, but you knew you didn't have to worry anymore with a parent present. That's what God's presence did for me; it was as if He brought a flashlight and sat next to me. Nothing would mess with me as long as He was there.

And with that sense of relief came the ability to adapt to my current reality as best I could and then simply accept what I couldn't change. Everything was ultimately out of my hands at that point, as I quickly learned.

That first chemo treatment took almost five hours from check-in to dismissal. Around lunchtime, I was absolutely starving. I had skipped breakfast that morning, since I wasn't sure how I would be feeling after my treatment, but three hours in, my stomach started gurgling really loudly. I was excited to see there was a Boston Market right across the street from Hillman because I was a big fan of their food, and since I still had another two hours or so to go, my mom left to pick up lunch. When she walked back in with rotisserie chicken, sweet potatoes, macaroni and cheese, and corn bread, I started to think that maybe twelve sessions here might not be so bad after all.

There was just one issue for which I had not accounted: my body was getting pumped full of two IV bags of *poison*. No amount of good intentions could convince it not to do what bodies are meant to do when they detect poison: get rid of it. First, I threw up my rotisserie chicken. The sweet potatoes followed. Then the corn bread decided to come back up to say hello, and suddenly I realized that this whole chemo thing was going to be a lot harder on my body than I'd expected. The chemo didn't care that I was in peak physical shape or was excited to enjoy a delicious meal; its only job was to wreak havoc on my internal organs and destroy the cancer. And that's what it did.

After that, I was afraid to eat at any of my other favorite restaurants after my biweekly "chemo fast," no matter how much I was craving them, because I didn't want any other beloved eatery to be ruined for me the way Boston Market now was. Two weeks later, when we drove past Boston Market on the way to my second chemo treatment, I had to close my eyes because just the sight of the sign made me feel queasy. My brother Michael, who had taken leave from the Air Force and flown up from Florida to be with me, was sitting in the backseat. He gave me a funny look as I started groaning.

"What's up, J? You love that place," he said.

I just shook my head. "I can't go back, man."

We started taking a different route for my next appointment so we didn't have to drive by that restaurant.

In fact, as the weeks went on, I started to develop more reactions that required me to adapt instead of obsessing over them. The second week I began dry-heaving as Sarah connected the IV bag; it was almost as if my body knew what was coming and was bracing itself for attack. Once I realized that this was going to be a regular thing, I prepared myself for the instinctual response and practiced slowing my breathing so I could ride the wave of the nausea. There wasn't much I could do to stop the heaving, but at least I could prevent the misery from causing me to spiral emotionally.

When I was given the saline rinse in my port catheter to prepare me for the IV, I started to develop a horrible metallic taste in my mouth. The flush would start, and suddenly I felt like I was sucking on a mouthful of pocket change. But instead of worrying myself about it every week, I just tried to combat it with a handful of Jolly Ranchers. Unfortunately, nothing worked, but I kept at it, cycling through grape, cherry, green apple, watermelon—anything with a strong fruit flavor. As the metallic flavor started lingering, lasting for hours and then for days between treatments, I reminded myself that

I was choosing not to stress over the things I couldn't control and simply adapt as best I could. Those little efforts were small things, but they allowed me to feel like I was still doing *something*. I wasn't completely checked out from my own life or treatment, but I wasn't trying to micromanage it either. I was adapting to and accepting things as they came.

Together, these three steps became my road map for rejecting fear:

1.   Educate yourself so there aren't as many unknowns, but acknowledge that you can't be ready for everything.
2.   Let go of whatever isn't serving your best interest.
3.   Adapt until you can't—then roll with the punches.

I'm not claiming this is a magical secret or deep wisdom for eliminating worries. I didn't learn about these steps from any kind of ancient writings or self-help sage; I simply committed myself to finding an alternative to fear. As I did so, I paid attention to what worked, and these became the practices I tried to stick to throughout the whole experience.

While in treatment, I continued to live my life as normally as possible so that fear would not get the upper hand. Of course I followed my doctors' advice, but I also did not treat my body as if it were fragile, broken, or needed to be babied. I continued to go to school and showed up every morning at 4:15 a.m. for all team practices. I participated in every workout and ran every drill along with my teammates exactly as I would have if I was completely healthy. The only difference was that I had a mask on to help protect my compromised immune system and carried a Gatorade bottle with me so I could spit when the metallic taste became overpowering. I showed up on time for the weight room and waited my turn to bench press along with everyone else. If I felt like I might be sick during practice, I discreetly went inside until it passed; I didn't want to be a distraction or draw attention to myself by throwing up on the sideline. I educated myself on what I could and could not do; I accepted my vulnerabilities and limitations without using them as an excuse, and I adapted to my circumstances in order to continue reaching each small goal I set as I aimed to rebuild my future.

I also refused to let go of my faith. Fear is a choice and so is faith; we can choose to believe in a higher power or we can choose to believe it's all on us. Personally, I'd rather know someone else is there, walking beside me, than to have to carry the burden all on my own. If God is who He says He is, I have no reason to be afraid, because He is bigger than whatever issue I am facing anyway. My job was just to keep living and working toward my goals and aims as best I could; if my biggest fear was that the disease would end my dreams, I wanted to fight back by pursuing those dreams even harder.

A month or two after my final chemo treatment, during a seven-on-seven summer practice game, I caught a 35-yard pass in the end zone. That catch meant nothing in terms of my record or stats or highlight reel or anything an NFL scout might see, but it meant everything to me. *I'm back! I'm back!* The thought kept racing through my head. I pointed up at the sky, like I try to do after every touchdown. *Thank you, God,* I thought. *You are the reason I am standing here now—not just in the end zone, but on this earth. I don't know what You have in store for me, but I know You walked me through this whole ordeal for a reason.* That moment proved to me that my dreams were not over.

Standing in the end zone with the ball in my hands and the hot sun shining down on me just six months since I'd been told my life was in danger, I knew I'd made the right decision. My choice was victory, not fear. It may not have been on my timeline, but that's because God was still working, and I had to decide to trust Him.

By taking back my power, I was able to give cancer the fight of my life and attacked it just like I would any opposing team. My football coaches taught me to leave everything I had on the field, and I decided that I was going to fight with every last bit of strength to do the same in my battle with cancer. By rejecting fear and embracing hope, I was able to face the most frightening period of my life with more calm and courage than I realized I possessed.

Ultimately, though, I knew as a Christian that death had no power over me because of the sacrifice of Jesus. Human fears mean nothing in the long run because God has already won the game of life and death for us. That realization gave me hope and confidence that my life would have significance no matter how it ended, but I also had faith that God had more in store for me—that He wouldn't let my story stop here.

Life is always going to give us periods full of uncertainty and instability. It could be facing down a three-hundred-pound lineman, or it might be a difficult diagnosis or the loss of a job or a shift in a relationship or a challenge to your faith. Whatever you are facing today, I encourage you to remember that fear *is* a choice. Feeling fear does not mean you have to live in fear. You can take deliberate action to choose to move away from your worries and toward behaviors that will serve your ultimate purpose more fully. Fear does nothing to improve your life or build your dreams. And patience, endurance, and determination will get you a whole lot closer to your target than fear will.

We can't know exactly what's waiting for us down the road; even the best map can't show us exactly what lies ahead on our journey—detours, potholes, unexpected delays. Fear lives in the unknown, but here's the catch—*so does God*. We don't know what the future holds, but God does. When we take a step back and remind ourselves that fear is a choice, we can commit ourselves to working *through* the unknown—whatever form that work takes.

CHAPTER 6

THE MENTAL GAME

"Why are you doing that?" one of my teammates asked. "Don't punish yourself."

I was concentrating too hard on the video on my phone to notice he'd said anything.

"J!" he repeated. "Are you sure that's a good idea?"

I popped my earbuds out. "Sorry—what did you say?"

"Never mind." He shook his head and picked up the magazine he'd just put down.

I scrubbed the video on my phone back a few seconds to rewatch what I had missed and tried not to look at the IV bag that was pumping chemo meds into my chest as I settled back into my chair.

The highlight reel started again, and I watched myself weave down the field, leap up and over the dogpile at the goal line, and soar right into the end zone. It was hard to believe that, barely over a year ago, those Duke defenders hadn't even seen me coming—and now I was hooked up to a machine that was poisoning me every other week in order to save my life. I didn't see *that* coming.

This was how I spent every other Monday, in the winter of 2015 and spring of 2016, sitting in a chemo chair, poring over YouTube videos and feeling miserable. Everyone hates Mondays. That's a universal, indisputable fact. Mondays are the worst. But I had an extra reason to hate Mondays because they were my chemo days. At first, I was grateful that the awfulness would all be contained to one day so my chemo didn't ruin several months of perfectly good Fridays, but the nausea, weakness, and weird bodily reactions to the treatment quickly became ever-present companions. There really weren't good days and bad days—more like bad days and worse days.

The biggest challenge in a lot of ways, though, wasn't even the physical toll that the chemo took on me—it was the mental stress of feeling my body break down and knowing how hard I would have to work to build it back up again to my 2014 levels. All the while, my competition was getting that much better.

While I spent the previous season sitting on the sideline with my knee recovering, all the other Division I running backs were gaining more experience and more exposure week after week, game after game. Even as the college football season wrapped up in December, those guys would be spending the off-season working out, developing their skills, and generating buzz. Me? I'd still be glued to this chemo chair for the next six months.

I won't lie—there were times when I felt overwhelmed by the unfairness of it all. All my life I'd been fighting to prove myself: to be part of the big kids' games, to be a starter, to be part of the discussion. I rooted my work ethic in proving myself. I wanted to show everyone around me that I deserved to be there even if I was smaller/younger/not as heavily recruited. Now I had been forced out of the competition for something that was completely beyond my control. I wasn't being benched for not meeting academic standards or for getting into scrapes with the law; I was falling behind because something awful happened *to* me.

Thankfully, whenever I began sinking into an emotional slump, someone or something pulled me out of it pretty quickly. The amazing support from my family and friends helped me immensely, and I also found strength in the very clear vision I held of myself beating this disease. I allowed myself—and sometimes forced myself—to keep that vision at the forefront.

Of course, my major aim was to make it to the NFL; that was the top of the mountain for me. But that aspiration also felt overwhelming at times. How could I hope to make it to the NFL when there were days I couldn't even make it up a flight of stairs without stopping to catch my breath?

As I wrestled with that question, I learned to recognize the difference between goals and targets. People love to talk about the importance of setting goals, as if a goal is the ultimate reason to do something—"Finding your *why*" as it is commonly referred to. What endpoint are you trying to reach, and why does it mean so much to you? In my experience, focusing on the big picture can actually make things seem more overwhelming. I actually see the big *what* and *why* as your target. When you aim yourself in a specific direction toward a target, all of your preparatory actions come together to guide you toward your ultimate destination.

The challenge with calling this endpoint a "goal" is that things rarely play out exactly the way we envision them, and it's easy to feel discouraged, impatient, or frustrated with the process. (And I have some firsthand experience with disrupted plans.) People love to say, "The journey matters more than the destination," and I understand their point. But what if your journey takes you in a different direction? You've got to have a clear sense of your destination or else you can easily end up off course or burned out. If your journey takes some unexpected turns, follow where the road leads you, but don't lose sight of your purpose. If we instead think of that focal point as our *target*, it allows us the flexibility to go toward our destination without feeling we missed the mark completely just because unforeseen circumstances altered the path. A goal is a precise, specific accomplishment. A target is a more generous window for success that acknowledges that some of the details are out of your hands.

In contrast, I like to view goals as the milestones along the way that help me toward my aim. For example, I set the goal of making it through my first chemo treatment. When that was behind me, I set my sights on the halfway point. I created goals of completing a workout or even just pushing through the dry heaves I got each time the IV bag was connected. As I reimagined the way I set goals, I began to build up a personal sense of momentum. *One goal down!* I gained a sense of accomplishment with each milestone I marked, as well as a sense that I had just moved that much farther down the road toward my target. Even though I knew my ultimate driving force was to play football again and make it to the NFL, I felt overwhelmed when I compared where I was at that moment to where I needed to be. If the NFL was my goal, it felt hopeless. But if I instead shifted my thinking to make that my target—the eventual point toward which all my preparatory actions were pointed—I could focus on achieving the series of smaller but necessary steps in that direction.

Of course, one of the biggest challenges was that all those smaller but necessary steps were pretty limited. I continued to attend every practice and training session during chemo, but nothing could make up for the playing time I had lost on the field the previous fall, not to mention the physical strength that had deteriorated. Rather than giving up, I decided instead to focus on the mental game. I watched my highlight videos obsessively to study what had worked best for me when making big plays and tried to relive those moments in my head. I would close my eyes and imagine the sound of the crowd, the smell of the grass, and the feeling of the air. I would see the field in my head just as I had seen it on game day, and then I would reenact the play. It was a way to create muscle memory without moving a muscle.

Each time I re-created a specific drive, I tried to commit every detail to memory. I relived the sights and sounds of the crowd. I imagined my legs pushing hard off the ground so I could jump to exactly the right height in order to make the catch, the feeling in my knees and ankles as I landed safely back down. I thought about stretching out my arms, the sensation of wrapping my fingers around the ball as I made contact, the impact of the ball against my chest as I pulled it in tightly. It was like watching game reel in virtual reality, frame by frame—sometimes in real time, sometimes in slow motion, but always in a way that told my brain: *This is real. You can do this. You have done this. You will do this again.*

Each time I relived a great play on the field, I felt my body reacting excitedly to do it again. Rather than obsessing over what I couldn't do right now, I chose to focus on what I did in the past and what I planned on doing again. I didn't want to limit myself with my own self-doubt. I knew that, once I came back, there were going to be people coming out of the woodwork on social media to offer their unsolicited opinions—especially the first time I didn't get 100 yards or score a touchdown in a game. Sure enough, that's exactly what happened during the first game or two the following season. But by that point, I had come to realize that my contribution to my team was more important than generating hype for myself. I knew what I was capable of before my treatment, and I was even more aware of what I was capable of after it. My body had been through hell and still made it through to the other side. Compared to that, running a ball into the end zone was nothing.

During treatment, I couldn't stop myself from watching the highlight reels of my opponents—the guys I knew I would be up against in the draft. At first, I was worried about how good they were getting with each passing game. But then I reminded myself that I couldn't change my current circumstances, so I might as well figure out how to use those circumstances to my advantage. Instead of sweating over how sharp some of those guys looked on the field, I decided to study their techniques to see what tips I might be able to pick up. After all, if I was going to be stuck in a chair for hours on end, I should use it as research time.

I dove into those videos, dissecting them and pinch-zooming to analyze footwork and technique. Instead of studying the entire defensive line of an opponent, as I would have done with game tape ahead of a matchup with a rival, I zeroed in on just the running backs. I tried to imagine acting out each of the plays on their highlight reels just as I would imagine my own—the linemen I faced, the conditions of the field, the game philosophy of each coach. *What would I have done differently on that play? What did the other run-*

ning back do that might not have been instinctual for me but clearly worked in that situation? As I worked through these questions, I gained insight into the game in a way I never had before. Certain moves that worked in one situation might not work in another; a running game against one team might have been disastrous against a different defensive lineup. West Coast teams sometimes had different playing styles than East Coast teams. I didn't just watch the other running backs I studied—I tried to *experience* the game as they had in order to figure out what made them so good. In my imagination, I stared down players I would never face in my college career due to conference schedules. It was an exercise in humility and a literal shift in perspective. Of course, I would have preferred to have been active that season, but since I couldn't change my situation, I changed my outlook.

The driving force behind all of this was a commitment to keeping my success in my sights. Every small goal reached, every inch of turf gained in the direction I was aiming, every game I replayed in my head was a success. I kept my eyes glued on what I wanted to achieve, and I celebrated each step along the way as a victory.

One of the clearest images I held in my mind was of our upcoming season opener against Villanova on September 3, 2016. That date was burned into my mind as the earliest moment I could be back out on the field. I spent countless hours imagining everything about my return to the field, a full year after this whole ordeal began with my torn MCL—back when an injured ligament was my biggest worry.

I created a movie in my head of what that game would be like. I imagined the uniforms we would wear—blue, since it was a home game—and what the grass would smell like (freshly mowed and painted). I imagined how the air would feel. I imagined the roar of the stadium as I breathed in the excitement and the noise and the energy, letting it fill my lungs and get my heart pumping. The fans, my teammates, and me—we were all there for the same reason: to kick off the best season of college football of our lives.

I went through every possible scenario I could imagine. I ran every route in the playbook, memorizing exactly where I needed to be and what my role was on each drive. I researched the Villanova defensive line and imagined what they would look like as I stared them down. I made that game as real in my head as I could possibly make it, living the game before I actually lived it. On the days when dreaming about the NFL felt too far away, this focus helped my aim seem more attainable. And that first game back against Villanova served as my driving force.

But as often as I replayed the movie in my head, there was still something missing. Despite imagining every detail with incredible clarity, it still wasn't as real as I wanted it to be. I wanted a tangible reminder of why it mattered so much. I wanted to make that game more than a movie, more than a fantasy. I wanted to remind myself that it was *real*, that it was something that was actually going to happen in just a few months, and that I was going to be there. So one night, when I needed a distraction from studying, I went online and designed myself a pair of custom cleats like the ones my brother had bought me my senior year of high school. When those shoes arrived in the mail a few weeks later, I turned them over and over in my hands, bending them to feel the way they flexed, and lacing them up to feel the way they hugged my feet. Then I put them up on my dresser where I could look at them and dream about the day I would finally get to wear them. *Watch out, Villanova. I'm coming for you*, I thought each time I walked past.

The cleats were white again, but instead of "King James" across the back in navy, this time I chose #24 embroidered in silver—a reminder that I'm not the king and not the One in control, as well as a reminder to always look for the silver lining. God is always working, even when we can't see it or don't recognize it at first. Devon Edwards, a tight end at Pitt, reminded me of this when he gave me a great piece of advice one day. "You're going to have a great story when this is all over," he told me. "God has already written a great story for you." That idea sustained me when I felt discouragement creeping up in the back of my head. *Is this really worth it? Can I really come back from this?* Those nagging whispers sometimes caught me off guard before I could fight them off.

Yes! I would counter. *God already has the ending in mind. I just need to stay the course and keep working toward what I think He's calling me to do.*

"It's already written," Dev reminded me whenever he saw me starting to get down. It never failed to make me smile. There was a great story unfolding; I just needed to be patient and not lose hope. The best way to do that was to keep my eyes fixed on what was ahead, so I made myself continue to look, to study YouTube highlight reels, to watch movies in my head of my first game back.

I also turned to the Bible and found a number of scriptures that reminded me of the importance of keeping my focus on what's ahead instead of where I might be stuck. Proverbs 4:25–26 says, "Let your eyes look straight ahead; fix your gaze directly before you. Give careful thought to the paths for your feet and be steadfast in all your ways." I loved the reminder to just keep putting one foot in front of the other, making the daily choice to keep pushing ahead. Meanwhile, Philippians 3:13–14 pulls the lens out to the big picture when it includes the line, "Forgetting what lies behind and straining forward to what lies ahead, I press on toward the goal for the prize of the upward call of God in Christ Jesus." Second Corinthians 4:17 even calls whatever trials we are facing in this life "our light and momentary troubles" that are nothing compared to "an eternal glory that far outweighs them all."

As I pored over these verses and others, I found myself thinking once again about the importance of perspective, and how grateful I was that I had developed a sense of it early in life. As easy as it was to let cancer loom large in my mind and dominate my thoughts, I needed instead to remain focused on what God was doing through this experience, and remember how relatively minor my illness was in the larger scope of my life. This challenge was nothing compared to everything I wanted to accomplish. I could dig into my disappointment, or I could choose to see my success.

That is the best advice I can offer anyone who finds themselves in a situation where they feel like their life has been put on hold and their dreams have been thrown into question. Don't focus on what you've lost or how far you have to go; focus on what it is you want to achieve in order to get to where you want to be. Recognize the process instead of obsessing over the outcome. When you can identify whatever the next thing is that needs doing—and then actually do it—you are making progress. Even if it feels like everything else has stalled out, simply doing the next thing is the bravest and best step you can take.

I knew what I wanted, and I made it *feel* real. I'm not advocating simple "mind over matter" thinking, but study after study has shown that visualization techniques, no matter what the situation—football field, boardroom, first date—can help the brain relax and feel more confident, which sets you up for success. The key is to have a very clear sense of what it is that you are aiming for and why. If you can fix your mind on the ultimate reason to keep pushing through, you will have a much easier time enduring the setbacks and heartbreak along the way.

This is why goals and targets are both important; you have to be willing to keep the destination *and* the journey in mind. You can't have tunnel vision on the endgame because you can't control the path. It doesn't matter how many to-do lists you make or how hard you work or how badly you want something to happen—you still can't predict the future. There will always be bumps you can't anticipate and twists you never saw coming. There will be situations that are nowhere near how you would have chosen your life to play out. But if you keep your aim in mind, you can continue pushing in that direction. Planning can carry you *to* a certain point, but perseverance and grit are required to get you *through* it. Circumstances rarely stick to the way we've scripted them in our heads, but if you can pick yourself up and face your new challenge without losing heart, you'll be that much closer to your target. When you can't have your first choice, focus on your second chance.

There are going to be times in life when you feel completely helpless—like all your options are gone, all your strength has been sapped, and everything you want is out of reach. When I was going through chemo, it was brutal to see other running backs in the conference continue to improve while my body slowly wasted away from my treatment. Instead of allowing myself to become paralyzed by fear or depressed by the progress of my competitors, I instead focused on what I wanted to do with my second shot at life and held that image in my head. I devoted all my energy to pursue that aim by setting small goals to act as markers along the way to chart my progress.

Sometimes a situation can seem so overwhelming that it feels impossible to see to the other side of it. If that's the case, don't exhaust yourself fighting to paddle to the top of that enormous wave; just concentrate on whatever the next thing is: *make it through today's treatment; take a shower; drive to work/school/practice; make it through the event without having to leave to throw up; make it to the bathroom before getting sick; get sick where you are but keep it off your shirt; get it on your shirt but vow that you will try again tomorrow* . . . You're going to miss some goals; that's inevitable and okay. The important thing is that you don't lose sight of your aim. Don't forget where it is you are ultimately headed.

In particularly trying times, it is more important than ever to stay focused and give yourself every possible reminder of why you have to keep moving forward. Make it real. Imagine what those moments look like, feel like, smell like, sound like, and taste like. Keep those sensations alive in your mind so that when the time is right, you will be able to come back better and stronger than ever. Staying focused on the *why* in the midst of painful circumstances and difficult situations can help us find the reserves of strength needed to keep fighting, even during the most extreme setbacks. Staying focused on the *how* can get us through the day-to-day grind. Why and how. The destination and the journey. The big picture and the daily steps to get there. Targets and goals.

Sitting in that chemo chair, I couldn't actually do a whole lot physically to work toward my goals, so I focused instead on the mental game. When I visualized what I would do on the other side of my illness, I didn't just see myself getting better—I vowed to become so good that the NFL wouldn't be able to say no. With both the short view and the long view in my mind, I set my sights on knocking down each goal on the way toward my target.

I still had a long way to go, but I knew why I was traveling and I knew where I was headed. There were times when that singular aim felt like the only thing I could be sure about—and on those days, that was enough.

CHAPTER 7

RECOGNIZE YOUR TEAM

Every two weeks, on Monday morning, when the winter sky was barely beginning to lighten and the piles of plowed snow were still frozen solid, my mom and I made the trek to the Hillman Cancer Center for my chemotherapy treatments. Moving through December, then January, and into February, my routine became as predictable as a western Pennsylvania winter: you may not know exactly what's coming, but it's going to be miserable.

Over the previous months, I'd tried very hard to keep my emotions to myself—not because I was trying to "play it cool," but because I just didn't see the need to create drama and pull other people into the ups and downs of my doctor visits. *Everyone has enough to worry about in their own lives,* I reasoned. *They don't need to worry about me, too.* Once I received my diagnosis, however, I had no choice but to share it publicly because word was going to get out sooner or later.

On the morning of my first treatment, two different people recognized me in the Hillman lobby and came over to talk. "You couldn't have kept this private if you wanted to," my mom whispered to me after I'd awkwardly smiled and stammered my thanks for their well-wishes. I was uncomfortable knowing that perfect strangers were now acquainted with my health situation—something that would normally be a very private matter. I appreciated the support I received from every corner, but it took a little while to overcome my discomfort with the attention and focus that the whole situation put on me. It seemed a whole lot easier to keep everything close to the vest and to work through it myself rather than making my treatment a community event. I know it takes a village and all that, but what did the village have to do with my personal health?

My mom, dad, and brothers could physically be present for me, but they couldn't actually feel what I was experiencing. No one could stand in my shoes, no matter how willing they were to do so. Any one of them would have traded places with me in a second if they could have—they all told me as much—but none of them could actually suffer the same panic over what was happening inside *my* body. None of them could feel the physical side effects I knew were coming after each chemo treatment.

I thought that I could combat the feelings of isolation by preparing myself to be as self-sufficient as possible during treatments; if I didn't need anyone else's help, maybe I wouldn't feel as frustrated or helpless. I quickly learned what to anticipate and how to tackle it. Before I even sat down, I made sure there was a supply of barf bags next to my seat so that I could grab one the moment I felt the nausea start. I also sweated profusely during the chemo, so I remembered to ask for a blanket each day before I got started so I wouldn't have to be soaking wet and shivering when I took off my dripping shirt.

One day, when Rich was sitting with me, I had already removed my shirt and was wrapped in the blanket when I felt myself beginning to get sick. Rich immediately looked around for a bag, but I lifted my arm to show him I was already holding one. As I leaned forward, heaving, Rich came around the chair and put his hand on my back. "Go wash your hand!" I croak-shouted in between heaves. "There's chemo in my sweat!"

Rich looked shocked, but quickly did as I told him. For my part, I just felt a hundred times worse. My brother was trying to be supportive and loving, but just touching me was hazardous to him. It was yet another barrier between us, making me feel separate from everyone else. James and his toxic sweat against the world.

Thankfully, this all changed fairly early in my treatments, when I was starting to get a sense of just how rough the road ahead was going to be. I glimpsed the concern on my mom's face as my new nurse, Kris, hooked up my IV bag. In an instant, I realized she would have gladly taken on all of my pain, but she couldn't. I struggled to express how awful everything in that moment really was. I know Mom wanted to understand what I was going through and wanted to do whatever she could to lessen my misery, yet the difference in how we were each experiencing that moment created a valley between us. My family had always been the one place where I felt completely and totally part of a whole. Now, because of something I had no control over, there was a huge, invisible divide between me and the people I loved most in the world.

Feeling totally alone, I glanced around the communal treatment area, where each patient sat in a kind of cubicle. Some people read newspapers while they sat, some watched movies, some talked with family and friends who had come with them. It wasn't always the same collection of people every day, since everyone was on different treatment schedules, but I still saw familiar faces. *They are in the same boat as me.*

What was more, I recognized the nurses who were checking on every patient; I thought about the exhausting shifts and unpleasant tasks they endured every day as part of their job, and how they never let on if they were hungry, tired, grossed-out, or unhappy. *They are here to make sure I'm doing okay.*

Dr. Stanley Marks, my oncologist, popped his head in to check on me between patient visits. Here was a man who dedicated his career not only to researching and fighting cancer but also to treating patients and their families with tremendous care and compassion. He answered every question Mom or I posed to him clearly and easily; his bedside manner made me feel relaxed, confident, and respected. *His focus is getting me the best possible outcome to this disease.*

The support staff was tireless, organized, and efficient with the administrative tasks, and happy to provide anything that would make my guests or myself more comfortable—a drink or a pillow or a better chair. They restocked the snack station and brought fresh supplies to each cubicle. And there was Rudy, the man who pushed the sandwich cart and loved to talk about Pitt football; he started working at Hillman because his daughter had suffered with cancer years before and he wanted to make sure he could offer to others the same support and connection his family needed during that time. He had no reason to be there except that he wanted to pay forward the kindness his family experienced. *Their goal is to make me more comfortable.*

Even the treatment area itself was sponsored by one of Pittsburgh's favorite heroes. Mario Lemieux played hockey for the Penguins for seventeen seasons, including two Stanley Cup championships, and he is now one of the team owners. After his own diagnosis with Hodgkin's disease in 1993, Lemieux's foundation began investing in cancer research. In 2012, he sponsored the Mario Lemieux Center for Blood Cancers at Hillman.

Everywhere I looked, there was someone whose biggest concern was helping me and every other patient face our struggles with strength and dignity.

In an instant, my mind flipped from loneliness and isolation to a sense of community. Not everyone could understand exactly what I was going through, but everyone was committed to the same purpose: to defeat cancer. We were united by the same cause, regardless of our role: patient, family, friend, medical team, support staff, volunteer. Every single person was there because they wanted to beat the disease, and we were doing it together.

The moment I allowed myself to tear down those walls, I realized my team was so much bigger than I had imagined.

As a kid playing sports, I'd always heard about the importance of teamwork, but I'd always imagined that simply meant camaraderie and working toward a shared goal with the other guys in the same jersey as me. Now, I had a whole new perspective on who my team was and how each role could be wildly different—even while we all had the same end in mind. My team wasn't just some tight, select circle of the people directly impacted by my health; it was every person walking this walk with me in some way. And this team quickly became part of my biweekly routine.

Every other Monday morning at 5:30, my mom would drive down from Erie to pick me up at my apartment and take me to the Hillman Cancer Center's valet stand. It was an amenity offered for patients so we didn't have a long walk to get to the clinic, and it was a Godsend, as each week left me feeling weaker. The same three guys always worked the booth, and they'd take turns giving me fist bumps as I climbed out of the car. "Keep going strong!" they'd say as I walked inside. Just like that, my day started with a reminder that there were folks on my side.

I passed through the automatic doors and down to the elevator. "How are you doing?" another passenger would ask as we rode up. "I'm rooting for you."

The doors opened at the fourth floor—blood cancers—and there were Lauren, Theresa, and Faye smiling at the check-in desk as they always were. "Good morning, James!" they'd say. "What's your date of birth?"

"Five-five ninety-five," I'd answer.

"May 5 is a good day to be born," Faye would say, since we shared the same birthday. She'd then type my information into the computer.

"May 5, 1995. Good. Your birthday hasn't changed since last week," Lauren would laugh as she handed me my white wristband. "It seems silly to ask you every time, but hospital policy is hospital policy!"

"You guys are just doing your job," I'd say, putting on the bracelet. "Thank you!"

After sitting down, usually for only a minute or two, one of Dr. Marks's nurses—Julie or Kim—would call me back to check my weight and confirm I'd had a flu shot. I'm sure it was tedious and repetitive, but they never acted like asking the same questions was a nuisance; they listened to my responses as closely in week one as they did in week twelve. They'd make a note of everything on my chart, then Dr. Marks would come in and ask a few more questions—"How are you feeling? How is your appetite? How are you sleeping?"—while he felt my neck and armpits to see if I had any swollen lymph nodes. In the meantime, the staff would check with my mom to see if she had any questions or concerns ahead of that week's treatment.

Then it was off to the back room for the blood draw—six tubes each time—and a ten- to fifteen-minute wait while they analyzed the samples and determined the precise mixture for my chemotherapy that session. Meanwhile, the nurse would access my port, apply the numbing cream, and get the tubes ready to receive the chemicals— which meant they had to run the saline flush that caused that dreaded metallic taste. When that was done, she would step out for a few minutes and return wearing the huge blue apron and gloves. She'd hook up my first IV bag of whatever the poison soup of the week happened to be and make sure it was flowing as it should. The routine was always the same.

It was predictable.

It was completely uneventful.

It was exactly what I needed.

There was nothing exciting about my treatment days; I had no reason to look forward to yet another week of nausea and weakness. But showing up each time was, weirdly, a joy, even though I absolutely dreaded the treatment itself. From the moment I stepped out of the car, I knew everyone at the Hillman was on my side, cheering me on as I endured treatment after treatment. Their job was to make sure that the patients had whatever support they needed in order to fight their disease however they needed to.

There is profound power in helping someone face their challenges head-on, both for the person assisting and for the person going through the ordeal. For the supporting community, the feeling of purpose and being part of a whole can be deeply fulfilling. It would be easy for any one person to say, "My role isn't that important. This team could function fine without me." But the truth is that a team needs every member in order for the unit to perform at its best. What impressed me at Hillman was that everyone seemed to have a clear sense of purpose—of how their work contributed to the shared mission. Doctors and nurses weren't the only people who found value in what they did. The people who worked in the lobby and helped direct people to the right floor played an important role. The three ladies at the front desk who checked me in with smiles on their faces made me look forward to the beginning of each day. The servers in the cafeteria and the crews who mopped floors when someone got sick served a larger goal. It wasn't just that they did their jobs—it was that they did their jobs *with purpose*. The entire center functioned as a cohesive unit. Each patient was an individual, but we weren't alone; every single person there was part of a seamless whole. There was one major objective, and each member contributed to the overall success in his or her unique way, whether it was treating the disease, supporting the treatment, taking care of practical details—or sitting in the chair, receiving the chemo, and doing the fighting.

My experience with my amazing health-care team reminded me of the passage in 1 Corinthians 12:15–20, where Paul writes about how essential each part of the body is to the overall health of the individual:

Now if the foot should say, "Because I am not a hand, I do not belong to the body," it would not for that reason stop being part of the body. And if the ear should say, "Because I am not an eye, I do not belong to the body," it would not for that reason stop being part of the body. If the whole body were an eye, where would the sense of hearing be? If the whole body were an ear, where would the sense of smell be? But in fact God has placed the parts in the body, every one of them, just as he wanted them to be. If they were all one part, where would the body be? As it is, there are many parts, but one body.

One body. One shared vision. One aim. But the full strength that a collection of people, talents, knowledge, and skills brings can only be unleashed when the person going through the struggle *recognizes their team.* It's a whole lot easier to face a battle if you know you have an army behind you—an army trained in all the different ways you probably aren't. The medicines may work and the cancer may be eradicated, but unless you are able to recognize the incredible collection of people around you, you will continue to believe you are fighting on your own. And if, God forbid, the cancer cannot be defeated, it's much more empowering to face what's coming if you know you have a community of people who are standing with you, pulling for you, and crying with you. Battling an illness may be an individual act, but it doesn't mean you have to face it alone. The cancer journey is different for everyone, but we all need a team on that journey with us.

I understand that it can be hard to push past the barriers between isolation and community. There can be any number of reasons why a person fails to recognize their team. It could simply be a matter of habit—individuals who have gotten used to doing things on their own may see no reason to change that now. It could be pride—they don't want to admit that they need help from anyone else. It might even be embarrassment stemming from a desire to avoid others seeing them at their weakest. In my case, it was probably a little bit of most of those.

But sitting in that chair, completely helpless, I realized that I had to rely on other people. From mixing the chemo meds to hooking the bag up to filing the insurance paperwork to simply getting myself a bottle of water—there was no way I could do any of that alone. What was more, *I didn't have to.* How ridiculous would it have been to try to take everything on myself when there was an entire team who wanted to help and was specially trained and equipped to do so? I even had people who were taking time away from work and school and other responsibilities for the sole purpose of making sure I didn't have to spend those days by myself. What an incredible gift that was! So what if they couldn't feel what I felt? When a team runs a play on the field, everyone has a different job. The quarterback has to call the play, the center has to snap the ball, the blockers have to block, the running backs have to run . . . Everyone has their own job to do, and only one player can have the ball at any given time, but that doesn't mean they don't all have the same goal. I just needed to recognize the people around me for who they were—my team. It was just the playing field that was different.

It was quite a surprise when I discovered that not only did I need every member of my health-care and support team to help play their part in my treatment and recovery, but I also started to look forward to seeing them each time I went in for treatment. I still go back to Hillman every six months for blood draws and a chest X-ray, just to be sure the cancer hasn't returned, and each time I go, it's like a family reunion. I get to see so many people who are *still* in the fight with me, even years later. They are excited to see me because my life is proof that their effort made a difference to me. I love catching up, asking about what their kids are up to, or seeing photos of new grandbabies. I still get text messages from Rudy with the sandwich cart, checking in to see how I'm doing or wanting to shoot the breeze about Pitt football. Dr. Marks has pretty much become family to me. All of these people are now part of a bigger network I would have never known except for the terrible experience they helped walk me through. I never would have chosen to travel this path, but I'm awfully grateful for the people who decided to walk beside me.

When we go through difficult times, it can seem as if we are totally alone, but we never are. God always seems to find a way to put at least a few people in our paths who are our allies. They may not be with us every second of the day or even every step along the way, but you can usually find someone who is rooting for you if you look hard enough and let down the walls you may have put up. Relying on others can often be one of the hardest things to accept when going through a challenging time—especially if you are a super-independent person like me—but it can also be one of the most rewarding. You just have to be willing to allow yourself to be a part of the community that has already formed around you.

When I first started my chemo treatments, the schedulers at Hillman offered me my own room, in case I wanted to maintain some privacy. I deeply appreciated their offer, but I declined. I wanted to be present with all the other patients who were going through treatment alongside me. The ability to look around the room and see other people hooked up to IVs helped me to feel a part of a community.

It's still important to continue to protect and recognize your personal boundaries, of course. Around treatment number six, when I started to get violently ill in the middle of my treatments, I did take them up on the offer of a private room. But up until that point, I wanted to have the visual reminder that I was not alone in this fight. I wanted to see my team, even if it was a very different team than I had ever imagined for myself—because it was one of the most important teams of my life.

What was more, I wanted to introduce that team to the other people in my life. When family, friends, or other football players would show up to support me, I wanted my visitors to meet the behind-the-scenes heroes getting me through this ordeal. I didn't want to have individual spheres of family and friends, football coaches and teammates, health-care team—all individual units with no overlap. Each person in my life who was willing to come with me on this journey was now part of a bigger team—and the more people I had around me to help me walk through this period, the better off I was going to be. Their compassion, love, and support helped me push away fear every day. Their presence made my battle seem less overwhelming. They reminded me that any worries only existed in my head—and I got to decide whether fear or faith dominated my thoughts.

In fact, just a few days after my initial diagnosis, Sean texted me a photo of the neck of his shirt pulled down to reveal a tattoo across his collarbone. His skin was still pink from the needle, but there in black ink read the words "Fear Is a Choice."

I knew Mr. Gallagher was strongly against tattoos, so I called Sean immediately. "Are you serious?" I asked him.

"Yup. I've got your back," he said. "I'm going to be there every step of the way. I wanted you to know that you don't have to go through this by yourself."

"Whoa. Thanks, man. But . . . is your dad going to kill you?"

Sean laughed. "He got one, too. It's on his shoulder."

"Wait—*are you serious*?" I asked again, nearly choking on the water I was drinking.

"Yup," he said. "I told you, we're all behind you."

A few weeks later, our buddy Carson got the same tattoo on his collarbone and Sean's little sister, Meghan, got the phrase tattooed on her back. My brother Michael got it tattooed on his stomach in February.

It was their way of telling me that I wasn't alone.

My army was so much bigger than just me, and fear didn't stand a chance against a team like that. They were bigger than any worries I might be feeling—and so was God.

The experience of suddenly finding myself surrounded by a new team changed me both as a person and as a player. By recognizing a broader team beyond just the guys next to me in the huddle, I realized that even though I was at the heart of *my* fight against cancer, I wasn't always going to be the person in the spotlight. Every day, someone else faces devastating news. Now that I know how it feels to have people rooting for me in something that *really* matters—more than a game, more than a trophy, more than a title—I want to do the same. I want to help others feel that same sense of shared strength and bravery when they need it. Sooner or later, everyone is going to come up against something that is too big to face on their own, and I want to be able to be part of their team when they do.

A lot of people put me first for a long time. It felt good, but it's also not a place where I wanted to get too comfortable. It's important to know when it's your turn to be at the center of things and when it's time to step back and rejoin the huddle. When you put other people first, you start to see them differently—you recognize their inherent value more. You start to see their worth not in terms of what they can offer you but simply on the basis of their humanity. Instead of focusing on what someone can do for you or what they represent, you start to appreciate them simply for who they are right now, in that moment. When you commit yourself to running alongside someone else, their hopes become your hopes. It's one thing to help someone accomplish their goals on the field; it's another thing to help them navigate through life.

Who is on your team? When you look around you, can you recognize a collection of people who share the same hopes that you do, and who all play some small part in your overall journey? It's easy to identify your team when all your jerseys are the same; it's not quite as simple when you are off the field, living in a world without clear, external markers to let you know at a glance who is on your side. In those cases, I would encourage you simply to run toward your target as hard as you can—but not so hard that you don't allow yourself to look to your left and right. Chances are, you will notice that there are people running alongside you. Who is putting your needs first during this period of your life? Who is adjusting their hopes and plans to better serve yours? Who is trying—maybe failing sometimes, but still trying nevertheless—to anticipate your needs? Who radiates positive energy? Who shows you empathy?

Who reflects compassion without judgment or even gives you tough love when you need it?

The more you are able to recognize the people who are walking beside you, in whatever capacity they can, the more grateful you will become for the allies you have, and the stronger you will feel. There is safety in numbers, and if you're willing to see it, you will probably be surprised by the number of people who are in your corner, fighting beside you, however they can.

Fear thrives on isolation; it loves to make you think you are weak, vulnerable, and all alone. The moments when I found myself battling the temptation to give in to fear were inevitably the moments when I felt like no one understood what I was experiencing.

Your team is limited only by where *you* choose to draw the lines. It can be defined as narrowly or as broadly as you decide. Even if you feel you have only a handful of people fighting for you, remember that they are just as valuable as a huge army, as long as you are in the fight together.

Your team is the heart and soul of everything you will ever accomplish and everything you are. When you are going through something deeply personal, it can be easy to retreat into yourself and focus on everything that seems to be resting on your shoulders. If you look around you, though, you will probably recognize people who are walking alongside you in a dozen different capacities. When we rally around one another during the challenging times, fear weakens and the fight gets easier. When you recognize your team, you start to understand that you are *not* alone, you are *not* isolated, and that fear is an illusion.

CHAPTER 8

SHOW UP

I shot Sean a look and he immediately stood up. "Thanks for dinner, but I think we should head out." If Sean's brother was surprised by our sudden departure, he didn't show it. He just walked us to the door and waved as we climbed into Sean's jeep. I buckled in and closed my eyes.

"Not feeling great?" Sean asked as he put the Wrangler into reverse.

I just shook my head.

Sean was so proud of that jeep. It was a 2001, but it was new to him; he'd only had it about four months, and he babied the heck out of it. Now that winter was over and the roads were clear, he didn't have to scrape the dirty salt and ice—road sludge—off the bottom after each trip, but he still kept it clean, both inside and out. A few weeks earlier we had gone out to a big, empty church parking lot where he had tried to teach me to drive stick shift, but I almost dropped his transmission and nearly ran into the side of the building.

I only nearly *hit it,* I thought. *I managed to stop in time. Barely. But I did stop.*

I tried to focus on positive things instead of my nausea as we bounced home through all the new potholes the winter had left behind. The Pennsylvania Department of Transportation wouldn't be able to repair them all until summer, and it made for a bumpy ride in the meantime.

"I can't believe you're almost through your treatments," Sean said as we pulled onto the highway.

"Yeah, eleven down, one to go," I sighed. "Hopefully." My voice sounded braver than I was feeling; the truth was, I was completely burned out from the chemo. It took a toll on my emotions as much as it did on my body. Even though my mom insisted that my hair was so naturally thick that no one else would be able to notice a difference, I knew it was falling out. Even if no one else could tell, I saw the clumps swirl down the drain each time I took a shower. I felt like I didn't recognize my own face in the mirror because my eyelashes and eyebrows had thinned out so much and the skin around them was puffy from water retention—another fun side effect of the treatments. I hated to shave; I joked that if I was going to lose all my hair, I shouldn't try to cut down the ones that were still growing. But the hair loss was nothing compared to the nausea, the constant feeling of exhaustion, and the sudden urge to be sick that could come without warning.

"Pull over, pull over!" I shouted to Sean, who immediately flipped on his right blinker. I felt the bile rising in my throat but was determined to *not* throw up in Sean's new jeep. A car slowed down to let us change lanes, and Sean punched the button to trigger the hazards as we reached the shoulder, but before I could open the door, it erupted.

There it was—the moment that broke me. "I'm sorry, bro," I said, when I was finally able to talk again. I tried to keep the tears from spilling—angry, frustrated, exhausted tears. "I'm so sorry."

"Don't worry about it, J," Sean reassured me. "Just get it all out of your system."

"But your car—"

"It doesn't matter," he said, smiling bravely at his ruined upholstery. "It's just a car."

I gave up trying not to cry. "I can't do this anymore, Sean. I can't face this again."

"You've only got one more treatment to go."

"But I don't know if I can do one more," I groaned, looking down at my filthy clothes. "I just don't know if I can."

"Just one more, then you're done," he said, wiping his own eyes. "Only one more and it's over. That's it. You can do this, J. You've got this."

We sat on the side of the road in Sean's jeep and cried together as the traffic sped past.

There are some friends who show up for the easy stuff, the fun stuff—the birthday parties and the housewarming dinners—and then there are the friends who Show Up for the hard stuff—the breakups and the moving days and the times when you are at your worst, physically or emotionally. In my case, sometimes both came on the same day.

As I'm sure you may have guessed by now, Sean is the second type of friend. Don't tell him I admitted this, but when we were in fifth grade, Sean was *incredibly* cool, while I was still a little awkward. I mean, one of my favorite people was Steve Urkel, if that tells you anything. But Sean looked past that and became one of my biggest encouragers. Throughout middle school and high school, he remained my best friend and biggest fan, even when he was the quarterback and star of our team and I was a second-string running back trying to get noticed. He was always advocating for me with the coaches and telling me not to give up. When we went away to college, he got a scholarship to play football at Edinboro University, about twenty minutes away from Erie, but we still hung out whenever we could. When I introduced him to my teammates at Pitt, I always said, "This is my brother, Sean." Even though we look nothing alike, no one ever questioned it.

After my diagnosis, when I realized I needed to make a formal announcement to the media, Sean and Mr. Gallagher came down and helped me write it—no hesitation, no questions asked. They just hopped in the car and drove the hundred miles to Pittsburgh to sit up with me all night as we hammered out draft after draft. Despite Sean's classes and demands at school, he continued to make the drive to Pittsburgh almost every other week after that to sit with me during treatment or drive me to appointments.

And Mr. Gallagher even came to my treatments a couple of times to take photos and video of the journey.

"You're going to want to see this someday," he told me, "to remind yourself of what you are capable of overcoming. And when you are drafted into the NFL, your team is going to want this for their human-interest piece on you."

"Why are you Gallaghers so good to me?" I joked one time.

Mr. Gallagher just shrugged. "You showed up for Meghan."

Our senior year of high school, when Sean's sister Meghan was a sophomore, she was diagnosed with a kidney disease. Her condition meant she was often stuck inside the hospital for extended stays. Sean and I frequently drove to Hamot Medical Center in downtown Erie to keep her company and let her parents have a break to talk with the doctors, grab a bite to eat, or just take a shower. Meghan loved to see Lake Erie out the window, but she was often too weak to walk down the hall to where the best views were, so I would scoop her up and carry her down to the big picture windows so she could see the sunset and take photos of the water. I started volunteering with the National Kidney Foundation after that because I gained a new appreciation for what patients and families go through as they face the challenges of a life-altering diagnosis. I didn't think anything of it at the time; it just seemed like the right thing to do with the health and energy that I'd been blessed with. Meghan was like a little sister to me, and I knew she was going through a rough time. If I could help cheer her up and make her family feel supported, that's what I wanted to do. It's what the Gallaghers had always done for me. And I guess that's how showing up works: you just start meeting people where they are until it's the most natural thing in the world to be by their side when the bottom drops out on their lives.

What I learned from that is the importance of Showing Up— capital S, capital U. We all have unspoken rules in our relationships— how much we give; how much we ask for; how much time, effort, and emotional capital we feel we can invest. Most of the time, we keep those healthy boundaries in place in order to maintain balance and order in our lives. But sometimes there are circumstances where we know in our bones that the right thing to do is to Show Up for someone, wherever, whenever, however we can.

Showing Up doesn't have to look like any kind of a grand gesture or major sacrifice; it's simply being present in a capacity that meets a need. It might be as simple as picking someone up from a medical appointment or as big as sitting with them as they wait for a diagnosis. It could be folding laundry for a friend when they are completely overwhelmed or attending their dad's funeral even if you barely knew him. It's not about the gesture itself so much as it is about the recognition that someone has a need you can meet—and then following through. Often, we say, "Let me know if you need anything," and the conversation ends there. People tend to be reluctant to pick up the phone and actually take someone up on that offer. Don't wait for someone to come to you with a need! Bring them dinner if they're sick. Mow their lawn if they've broken a leg. Call and say, "I am at the store right now; what can I pick up for you?" Help is inherently active, not passive. You need to actually *do* it—whatever "it" may be. Showing Up is about having skin in the game, even when the game isn't yours. It's not tied to guilt or obligation; it's born out of love, loyalty, and empathy.

This isn't something you can do every day or for every person you meet. It's impossible (not to mention impractical) to Show Up for every single person in your life, every single time they go through a rough patch. The ability to say "no" to others sometimes is incredibly important, too. But when Showing Up is the right thing to do, you just know.

And it matters. Oh, believe me, it matters.

My mom came to every treatment. Every. Single. One. She drove all the way from Erie to Pittsburgh, two hours each way, every other week, just so she could be there for me each time I went in for chemo. She knew I was surrounded by coaches and teammates who weren't going to let me be alone, but she was in full-on Mama Bear mode, and her son was *not* going to have to face fighting cancer without her there. For the first couple of treatments, until I felt confident that I could handle the effects of the chemo on my own, my coaches paid for a hotel room so my mom could stay with me. That might seem like a small gesture, but it was actually huge for my family. That hotel room allowed me to have extra help when I wasn't yet sure how I would manage, but it also meant Mom didn't have to make the 260-mile round-trip drive in one day. She already worked two jobs and had to take extra time off both of them to be with me. Just having someone cover the cost of her room helped lighten her burden. My mom Showed Up because that's what moms do, and my coaches Showed Up to help make that possible. That support lifted a huge weight off my shoulders.

My mom also Showed Up for me when she picked up the phone and called my dad to tell him about my diagnosis. When I first found out, I was overwhelmed by the news and not quite sure how to put it into words, so the thought of telling my dad about it was more than I felt I could handle. My dad is someone who likes to take action, so I knew he would want to ask questions and discuss options exhaustively, and I simply didn't have the emotional capacity to navigate all of that just yet. When I asked Mom if she could call him and let him know, she asked if I was sure I didn't want to tell him myself. When I explained why I didn't feel up to it, she immediately agreed and made the call, which gave me one less thing to worry about. And my dad Showed Up, too. He swapped shifts in order to come with me to a chemo treatment. I'm sure the appointment was tough for him to watch—there is nothing you can really do but sit and wait while the IV drips—but he wanted to be there with me, and it meant the world to me. We both knew there was nothing more he could do to help my situation, but he gave me his time and attention, which spoke volumes to me about the depth of his love.

My brothers also followed suit. Glen, Rich, Michael, and Rico all took turns coming to my treatments, rearranging their work schedules and coordinating with one another so they could each go with me to treatment at least once. It wasn't easy for them, especially since they didn't all live in Pittsburgh. Michael was in the Air Force at the time and was stationed in Florida, yet he took leave and came home just to make sure that I knew he was right there in the fight with me, even if he couldn't be physically present all the time. If he hadn't made the trip, I would have completely understood and never would have held that against him in a thousand years. But he made the effort to Show Up and be with me during my second treatment, and it is still the best gift he has ever given me.

Even my grandmama made arrangements to sit with me twice, which was especially meaningful since she had recently gone through breast cancer treatment herself and wasn't yet back to 100 percent. But she was determined to be there, holding my hand and praying with me. Even though she knew she couldn't make the disease or the physical pain go away, her time, presence, and love gave me a sense of comfort that nothing else could. It wasn't convenient and I know it wasn't comfortable for her, but she never once complained. She never made anything about herself; she made sure everything was focused on my well-being. That's what Showing Up is: giving of yourself in order to help another person.

Rob Blanc, the head football athletic trainer at Pitt, went with my mom and me to all my diagnostic appointments. He was there for the biopsy. He was there when I got the confirmation of lymphoma. He gave us his personal number and told me to call him anytime, day or night. Of course, lots of people say, "Call me anytime," but most of them don't actually mean *any*time. Rob did. "I don't care if it's two o'clock in the morning; I'll keep the ringer turned up all the way," he promised. "You call me if you need anything at all." Thankfully, I never had to, but it meant the world to me just knowing that I could, and that Rob would really and truly Show Up if I needed him to, day or night.

My family and my closest friends did everything they could to lighten my load and make me feel supported, cared for, and encouraged. It would have been a lot easier for them just to send me some cards or pray for me from a distance—and those are really wonderful things that I would have appreciated. But they Showed Up for the bad times. They were there when I smiled through the nausea in order to take photos with fans who spotted us when we were out in town. They were there when I gave myself pep talks in the mirror just to get myself out of the house that morning. They were there during a particularly terrible night, when I cried and confessed, "I don't know if I ever want to wake up again." I know there were times when they felt helpless, hopeless, or even just awkward about not knowing what to say. They may have even wrestled with being too afraid to do anything for fear of upsetting me, causing me stress, or saying the wrong thing. But the fact that they were truly there for me during my most difficult time taught me more about kindness, compassion, and love than just about anything I have ever known. They've seen me at my weakest, my sickest, and my most broken— *and they love me anyway.*

Through their example, the people closest to me helped me see what love looks like in action and, as a result, they helped strengthen my own belief in God. Because of the love shown to me by those around me, I now understand how Jesus changed the lives of the people around Him. Jesus didn't leave people where they were; he saw them at their lowest and still loved them. He engaged with them and made them better—physically, emotionally, and spiritually. Showing Up for someone is more than just dropping by—it's meeting them where they are and walking, sitting, or crawling with them, no matter the level of difficulty. Jesus lifted up and connected with the people around him through love and miracles. By loving each other fiercely by Showing Up, we can be miracles for each other.

When you commit yourself to being a person who Shows Up for others, you are, essentially, saying to those around you, "Being with you here and now, in the way you need me to, is the most important thing I can do." Think about what that communicates to your family and friends about their place in your life. What kind of dignity does that give to another human being?

Showing Up with an open hand, to play whatever role necessary, can be scary at times because you don't always know where things are going to lead. Sometimes, Showing Up for someone might even mean stepping into a position where they don't want you to help them. It might look like holding them accountable for damaging or self-destructive behavior or it might mean taking a hard line, even as you offer them a shoulder to lean on. It's not simply about being what someone wants you to be—it's about being who they *need* you to be, yet doing so from a place of love rather than a place of judgment.

Showing Up builds trust and breaks down barriers, and I think that is really at the heart of how we live out our faith. When you meet people at their lowest, worst, or most vulnerable and you show that you will stick by their side as they work through it—no judgment, just love—you show them a glimpse of God. It's at the heart of just about every Bible story about compassion—the Good Samaritan, Jesus healing the sick, Jesus eating with outcasts. For any person with strong religious convictions, or even just spiritual inclinations, Showing Up has to be one of the core tenets of life. I don't know of any major world religion that doesn't endorse showing kindness to those in need. It is part of what makes us human, and it is the best way I know of to live out your faith in a genuine way that shows others the beauty of your beliefs. As the famous expression goes, "People will forget what you said, people will forget what you did, but people will never forget how you made them feel."

Take the time to recognize who you can Show Up for in your own life and think about what you can offer that can meet a need. Just because you can't be physically present doesn't mean you can't Show Up. My friend Carson wasn't able to be in Pittsburgh for my treatments due to his schedule, but he constantly checked in with me or with Sean to see how I was holding up and if there was anything he could do for me. Showing Up isn't something determined by geography—it's about what you offer to someone that they can never repay. You can't pay back time; once it's gone, it's gone forever. You are literally giving someone a gift they can never give back to you.

I felt this keenly just a few days after I held my press conference announcing my cancer publicly when I received a phone call from Eric Berry, the Kansas City Chiefs safety who also had Hodgkin's disease. His video was the one I had shown my team when I broke my news to them, and suddenly, he was on the phone, asking me how I was doing.

He had heard about my diagnosis—someone actually slipped him a note during a team meeting to tell him a college player had just been diagnosed with the same cancer—and right away Eric contacted the University of Pittsburgh to see if he could get in touch with me.

We talked for more than half an hour that first day, discussing everything from symptoms and diagnoses to tips for training while undergoing treatments. I hung up the phone with a brand-new sense of empowerment. Someone else who had walked this same road reached back to coach me through it, too. He showed me I was worth the time and effort.

What impacted me most was knowing that this was absolutely not something that Eric had to do. We weren't from the same town. I didn't go to his alma mater. I certainly didn't have anything I could offer him. There was no reason at all that he should have made so much time for me . . . except that he saw a need in the world and recognized that he was uniquely positioned to speak to it. He invested so much of his personal time in mentoring me, helping me process my emotions, and giving me hope. Without even setting foot in the same room as me, Eric Berry Showed Up for me big-time.

We spoke by phone several times, and he texted me regularly to see how I was doing with the treatments. Every time we talked, I was humbled and amazed that this NFL stud would make time in his crowded personal and professional schedule to encourage a college kid he had never met before.

He didn't have to be in the same room or even the same city to Show Up. He made a huge difference on my outlook and attitude simply by taking a personal interest and following through on it. Eric made a personal investment in me when he had no reason to feel obligated to do so. Showing Up isn't about where you are, it's about what you do.

When things get tough, look for the people in your life who Show Up for you through the good times *and* the bad. Some people may let you down, while other people may surprise you by stepping up in deeply thoughtful and meaningful ways. The people who really Showed Up for me during my most difficult time are the heroes of my story. They made their own discomfort secondary to my needs at a time when I was at my lowest. The support they showed inspired me to be someone who Shows Up for others even in the worst of times.

Showing Up for the big things matters, and it's something we aren't called on to do very often. But showing up for the little things is important, too, and it is a choice we get to make every day. We can show up on time. We can have a good attitude. We can show up ready to work. As Steelers head coach Mike Tomlin likes to say, "The first step in getting better is showing up. You can't learn if you aren't there." Showing Up is the basis for building something that lasts, and each time we make the decision to be present, we are investing more of ourselves into the relationship, into the job, into the task at hand, into the common goal. Whether it's for an individual or a team, the way we show up matters and shapes everything around us.

Whatever it looks like for you, Showing Up is a good ground rule for living. It's not a decision you have to wrestle with. You know in your bones that you are supposed to be doing *something*, and you figure out how to do it. When it's time to Show Up for someone, you can sense it and you do it. Case closed.

When you Show Up (upper case) for the life-changing moments and show up (lower case) for the day-to-day responsibilities, it demonstrates that you are a person of your word, whether your word was "I'll be a contributing member of this team" or "I'll be there for you, for better or for worse." But what's even more important than that, it tells the people around you that you believe they are worthy of your time, attention, and best effort. It tells them that they matter. And I can't think of a more beautiful gift to bring to life than helping someone else recognize their own value.

CHAPTER 9

ENCOURAGEMENT MATTERS

The short flight from Pittsburgh to Annapolis didn't give me much time to think, which, given my current situation, was probably a good thing. The joy of Thanksgiving had been dampened by my possible diagnosis, and Christmas had been overshadowed by the start of my chemo. The lingering side effects offered a miserable preview of the next five months. The close of the football season should have meant preparing for the NFL draft, but that obviously wasn't happening for me this year thanks to the double whammy of my torn MCL and the small matter of the tumor wrapped around my heart. What else could I look forward to going wrong?

The mid-Atlantic sky in December is a distinct and unchanging shade of gray, and even though it was bright and sunny when the plane pushed briefly above the cloud cover, it was every bit as gloomy again when we touched down in Maryland. Pitt was headed to take on Navy in the Military Bowl on December 28, and even though I wasn't playing, I was still traveling with the team.

Because this year's bowl game was pretty close to home—only about 265 miles—we knew that Pitt fans were going to turn out in big numbers, excited to be tailgating in the nominally warmer temperatures of Annapolis and looking forward to what promised to be a great matchup. Sure enough, our fans did not disappoint— they were numerous and they were loud—but the game was ultimately a letdown. We lost 44–28. It was a painful loss to end the most painful football season of my life. I'm not going to lie: it stung.

As we left the tunnel and started trudging through the parking lot back to the team bus, I was surprised by the sight of a billboard-size yellow sign some Pitt fans had brought for me as a giant get-well card. That in itself was pretty impressive, but what really stopped me in my tracks was the fact that it was covered in signatures— roughly twenty thousand of them, in fact. Even though we lost the game, my teammates and I couldn't help but break into huge grins as we stood in front of this massive, sunshiny gesture of goodwill, emblazoned with the words "We are #ConnerStrong."

It was the "we" that really hit me. The signatures were from Panther and Midshipmen fans alike and were in no way tied to the game's outcome.

"James, can you pose with the sign so we can get a picture?" the Pitt media director asked.

"Sure," I said. "But how are we going to be able to get this back to Pittsburgh?"

"Just put it in your carry-on," someone joked.

In an instant, we went from a group of guys nursing a disappointing end to our season to a team reveling in the amazing support and love of our fan base *and* that of our recent rivals. That enormous card was not only a symbol of the incredible well-wishes and prayers of tens of thousands of people; it was also a reminder that football really is just a game, and there are bigger things at stake than a win or a loss on the gridiron.

We toss around the word *encouragement* pretty lightly in everyday life, but we don't always stop to think about just how powerful a word it really is. After turning it over in my head for a long time, it finally occurred to me that the word *courage* is right there in the middle of it. When I looked it up, I learned that's not a coincidence: *courage* comes from the Latin word *cor*, meaning "heart." In other words, *encouragement*, in its most literal sense, means to put courage into someone by building up their heart. When we offer encouragement, that's exactly what we are doing: we are cheering on a person's bravery and will to keep going despite circumstances, setbacks, or limitations. And when we foster that kind of strength in one person, we often end up fostering it in many more; a rising tide lifts all boats, after all. When one person gains a little more heart, everyone else tends to feel a bit stronger, too. Reaching out to lift up one person creates a connection that empowers them and enriches our own experience. Encouragement creates community.

From the moment Dr. Ferris told me I had cancer, my mom's mind spun as she tried to figure out how to help me feel loved and supported. She ordered purple rubber bracelets for lymphoma awareness, stamped with the words #ConnerStrong. She handed out those bracelets to probably half the population of Erie. All our family and friends wore them, but she also shared the bracelets with anyone who asked. She received messages on Facebook from people who wanted to know where to get a bracelet. People asked about buying them, but Mom didn't do it to make money; she was more concerned about getting people to pray and raising awareness, so she simply gave them away. Sometimes she even removed the bracelet she was wearing and handed it to whoever asked. "The more people know, the more people can pray," she insisted.

The first time I went home to Erie after my announcement, I was amazed to see all my friends and family wearing those bracelets. I couldn't believe that they would all choose to carry around a visual reminder of me on their bodies. What made me even happier, though, was when my mom would tell me she'd spotted a total stranger with a flash of purple on their wrist. She always figured out a way to get closer and take a look, and if she recognized it as one of my bracelets, she would thank them for their support. Several times she even spotted total strangers wearing the bracelets at the restaurant where she worked. Those moments, when she was reminded that so many people were pulling for her son and praying for her family, were like an energy drink for her soul. No matter how tired or worried she was feeling, she always felt a little better after spotting a #ConnerStrong bracelet. Encouragement for me was encouragement for her.

Encouragement does more than just lift up the person who is the target of it; it also gives a boost to those on the periphery—the caretakers, the support network, the folks behind the scenes—the people who give their time, energy, worry, resources, and love every day in order to show up for someone else. The daily grind of a major life event like cancer is exhausting for families, too; they may not have the disease themselves, but that doesn't mean it doesn't dominate their lives and their thoughts. "Just keep praying," Mom used to say each time someone asked what they could do. Whenever someone reached out to her to say that they were thinking of me, it was as if a tiny bit of the burden was lifted from her shoulders. She knew other people were lifting me even when she couldn't.

By figuring out a way to spread the word and generate prayers for me through those bracelets, my mom encouraged other people to think about people in their own orbit who were struggling. And when people took that message out with them into the world, my mom was strengthened in return by the reminder that her family was being covered in prayer. The people with whom she worked banded around her in beautiful ways as well. Her bosses at both jobs told her she could take off as much as she needed in order to be with me during my treatments, and her coworkers would offer her hugs and gift cards for gas to help with the cost of the two-hour drive down to Pittsburgh and back every other week.

That encouragement was greatly appreciated, because she was constantly worried about me. In all fairness, though, the worry was mutual: Mom fretted about me getting the treatment and support I needed, and I worried that she was taking too much on herself by driving back and forth from Erie to Pittsburgh so much. When I knew that my mom was being looked after—by her friends, by church groups, by my coaches, by people in the community who just wanted to show they cared—I had one less thing to worry about. I knew her emotional needs were being met and that her physical concerns, like buying gas and making dinner, were being thought of, too. That freed me up to focus wholly on my recovery. Each small act of encouragement, no matter who offered it, really did give us all a little more heart.

* * *

Just hours after I shared the news about my cancer at my press conference on December 4, I lay on my sofa in my apartment, trying to think about anything but the dread I was feeling and all the unknowns that lurked around the corner.

That evening was Pitt's big basketball game against Duquesne—the "City Game," nicknamed for the two big Pittsburgh universities who would duke it out at the Consol Energy Center. I would've loved to have been there, but my doctors warned me that my immune system would be compromised due to the chemotherapy, so I needed to start taking precautions. For the next few months, I would be confined to classes and practice, and even then I would have to wear a surgical mask to help reduce the chances of infection because even a common cold could wreak havoc on my body. Showing up to a game with nearly fourteen thousand other people was not exactly the best idea less than seventy-two hours before beginning aggressive chemotherapy.

I stretched out on the sofa, attempting to study for finals but getting more discouraged by the minute due to my inability to focus on anything worthwhile. Then, suddenly, my phone started to blow up with Twitter alerts.

Happy for the distraction, I picked it up and immediately realized there were dozens of tweets with the hashtag #ConnerStrong, which we had decided to use for my social media updates. I had just used it for the first time that afternoon. *Well, that caught on quickly*, I thought as I started to scroll.

Then I saw it—hundreds of fans in the student section wearing homemade #ConnerStrong T-shirts and holding up signs that read "I fight for _____," where they had written the names of people they knew and loved with cancer. In the front of the stands were a couple of huge banners on which they had written "We fight for James Conner."

My news wasn't even twelve hours old, and people were already turning up with shirts and signs they had made in their dorm rooms, standing together to cheer me on in a journey I had barely begun to walk. It seemed incredible, impossible, but picture after picture showed me that it was very real.

My body didn't feel any better, but my heart was suddenly a thousand times lighter. That day wasn't defined by sitting in front of a microphone, sharing tough news in a press conference; it was defined by the love and encouragement of my teammates and class-mates at Pitt.

Encouragement creates community. When those students arrived at the City Game with their shirts and signs and #ConnerStrong tweets, they were uniting for a cause. For that evening, at least, hun-dreds of people who may not have known one another came to-gether to share a message of hope and support.

Showing Up matters, but it's also not always possible. Not every-one is able to be present for every need that arises in a friend's or acquaintance's life; that would be exhausting and could easily con-sume every waking minute. It's important to recognize and protect your boundaries to reserve your greatest emotional investment for the people you love and who need you most. Maintaining that high level of engagement over an extended period of time is impossible; you risk burning out both yourself and the person you are trying to help. But there are plenty of other ways to show support that don't require as much personal and emotional investment and are much more sustainable in the long run. Encouragement can take countless different forms, and what's more, its impact often has a ripple effect.

There is something in fundraising circles called the "giver's high," which is a proven boost to feelings of happiness when someone performs a philanthropic act. I like to think that, at the most basic level, all the people who reached out to me also enjoyed a better day. This bleed-over effect of giving served the double purpose of not only cheering me up but also setting them up for a more optimistic outlook on the world. Their own kindness was returned to them.

In fact, I believe that the encouragement my teammates offered me helped us grow stronger as an organization. Despite early morning practices and full class loads to keep up with, my buddies would check with my roommate Rachid about stopping by our apartment to say hello to me. When a class let out early, I sometimes had visitors drop in to the cancer center to sit with me for a while. When a couple of local companies sponsored a biking event at Heinz Field, pledging to donate money to cancer research for each mile pedaled, about a dozen of my friends and teammates attended and rode as fast as they could so they could raise money while getting in a really good workout. The event wasn't linked to my diagnosis in any way, but the guys sent me pictures and texts from the event, letting me know they were dedicating their rides to me. I benefited from knowing my teammates wanted to do something in my honor. My teammates benefited from the bonding experience of shared goals. And other cancer patients would benefit because of the money they helped raise. Encouragement impacts everyone it touches.

I felt the outpouring of encouragement in a very real and direct way because of how it connected me with other people. In fact, even though I didn't realize it at first, I lived for those moments when friends reached out to me. When someone sent me a text message or a card to let me know they were thinking of me, it changed my outlook. Since I had to avoid crowds and big events due to my weakened immune system, I felt a bit cut off from the rest of the world. Getting those messages reminded me of the whole world that was waiting for me on the other side of this challenge. I loved those little reminders that someone was thinking of me in the moment, or that they had been thinking of me a few days ago when they dropped that card in the mail. I realized that I might be in someone's heart or in their prayers even when I had no idea they were thinking of me. We didn't need to be together for them to lift me up; even when I was physically alone, I knew I wasn't forgotten.

Encouragement created community for me, as I started to feel connected to the people around me in new and deeper ways. I knew that others were willing to give a little of themselves to lift me up, even when I couldn't offer them anything in return. They weren't reaching out because I was tearing it up on the field or because I had access to baller parties or because I was creating buzz about the upcoming NFL draft—just the opposite, actually. People were reaching out just because they *cared*. They couldn't do anything to make me better, but they *wanted* to. I heard from old friends I'd fallen out of touch with and acquaintances I barely knew from classes. I heard from *a lot* of people I'd never even met—local people who knew about my story, sports fans who followed college football, parents from five states away who didn't have any interest in my athletic career but who wanted to cheer me on in my fight anyway. They weren't sending me encouragement because they thought we might become best friends or because I could get them tickets to a game. They reached out to make sure I knew I wasn't forgotten just because I wasn't on the field. They wanted me to feel the combined power of their prayers. Their kindness and outreach gave me a little more courage to face each day.

Those acts of individual encouragement were beautiful and uplifting, and they helped me power through the day-to-day challenges, but sometimes encouragement can happen on a much bigger stage—literally. For me, the most surprising was probably when, on a perfectly ordinary spring day, I received a completely unexpected email. One of Ellen DeGeneres's producers contacted me, asking if I'd be interested in coming on the show.

Say what?

Having grown up watching the show after school, I firmly believed that *The Ellen DeGeneres Show* was one of the greatest things on TV—and now they were inviting me to dance my way onto the white couch next to Ellen? I stared at my screen in shock before totally freaking out. Yes, as a matter of fact, I would be *very* interested.

After several weeks of communication between the show, my coaches, my doctors, and me, we found a time that would work with my classes and treatment and with their taping schedule, and I flew out to LA for the episode. I'd never been to California before, and it totally lived up to expectations. I know I probably looked ridiculous grinning from ear to ear as production assistants drove me around the Warner Brothers lot, but I couldn't stop. Somehow, the physical misery felt a little easier to bear when I was surrounded by palm trees, warm sunshine, and the promise of hanging out with Ellen. I'd never been on national television before outside of game coverage, so it was a little weird going into hair and makeup— especially because I was so self-conscious about how thin my hair had become. But the crew did a great job making me feel comfortable as they powdered my head up into my hairline so I wouldn't be shiny on camera.

Standing backstage, I was reminded that I was welcome to bust a move when it was time to head out onto the set for my segment, but I decided I would try to keep my dancing to a minimum, the lingering memory of my torn MCL still haunting me. It was one thing to blow my knee on the football field, but it would be another thing entirely if I reinjured it while getting jiggy with Ellen. Besides, I was nervous and didn't want to do anything dumb. "I don't really have the moves right now," I explained, but I did still manage to embarrass myself, much to my brothers' delight. I was wearing a salmon-colored button-up, and as I raised my arm to wave to the audience, I showed the world my fresh pit stains. (That moment got replayed over and over for me when I got home.)

Ellen welcomed me and showed a short clip to introduce me to viewers, and then we chatted a bit about my treatments and my commitment to working out and practicing with the team even while I recovered. She mentioned that she heard I had been in touch with Eric Berry, and I confirmed that was correct and how gracious he had been with his time.

"Have you met him at all or no?" she asked.

"No, I've never met him," I said.

"I think you should meet him now," she said simply. "Eric, come on out."

The screen on the far side of the set raised, and there was Eric, smirking at the look of complete shock on my face. I stood up and wrapped him in the biggest hug I could, trying to communicate without words everything I was feeling in that moment.

All in all, that segment on Ellen was less than ten minutes of airtime, but it gave me a high that lasted for weeks. Ellen and her entire staff were unbelievably kind, generous, and respectful not only in how they welcomed me but also in how they considered my emotional needs. I thought I was just there to share my story and encourage other people who were going through tough times to stay strong. It's true—I was—but Ellen and her team also took that opportunity to encourage me by flying Eric in and reaffirming my own journey. On top of that, I felt connected to thousands—maybe even millions—of viewers who watched the program, and the clip soon went viral. Suddenly, people from all over the country were reaching out to me expressing their heartfelt thoughts and letting me know they were praying for me. I was overwhelmed by the love shown to me by complete strangers. This amazing, unexpected encouragement kept me going through my final chemo treatments, when I thought I couldn't take it anymore, when I was so nauseated I could barely eat. As my chemo treatments wrapped up in the following weeks, I was about as broken and exhausted as I could feel, but every time I thought back to that day, my heart felt warm. I often reminded myself, *You know, you've had some pretty amazing stuff come out of all of the awfulness.*

Amazing stuff out of awfulness. That sort of felt like my theme that semester. Encouragement can bring out the best in us, as I experienced firsthand with my professors that spring. I was enrolled for a full class load of fifteen credit hours, on top of the chemo, and I'll admit that I was a little nervous talking with my professors at the beginning of the semester, since instructors are under strict NCAA regulations not to give special privileges to student athletes. Thankfully, they all immediately recognized that I was not asking for favors but simply seeking accommodations for extenuating health circumstances. Every single professor was happy to work with me to adapt due dates to coordinate with my treatment schedule and the challenges of side effects; what was more, they all let me know they were pulling for me to beat the disease. Their desire to see me succeed not only in the classroom but in my fight against cancer, too, helped me begin the semester with an incredible sense of optimism that my life wasn't entirely on hold simply because of my illness. Their trust in me to stay accountable to my studies with an adapted schedule only made me want to work harder to reassure them that their trust was not misplaced.

It paid off when, one day early in summer practice, I opened my locker to find an envelope from the dean. I nervously tore it open. Was something wrong? Had I inadvertently missed an assignment or did I have to repeat a class? Trying not to panic, I unfolded the official letterhead and read the note congratulating me on making academic honor roll for the 2016 spring semester. It was too much; I had to sit on the bench as I read and reread that letter, grinning to myself at the amazing irony of it all. I had never made honor roll, and yet, somehow, in the midst of the toughest year of my life, I managed to earn the highest GPA of my entire academic career. That remains one of the proudest moments of my life.

Encouragement doesn't just challenge us to be a better version of ourselves in the moment, either; it can transcend the years. When I was a freshman at Pitt in 2013, Aaron Donald was one of our senior defensive tackles and the kind of guy we all wanted to be— ACC Defensive Player of the Year, a unanimous All-American, and a first-round draft prospect. Given the difference in our ages, he and I really didn't interact much until the final game of our one season together: the Little Caesars Pizza Bowl. Even though I was tearing it up on offense, the coaches wanted to slide me over to defense to see if I could make as big of a splash over there, too. That's when Aaron spoke up, "No. James, you need to keep running the ball."

He noticed me! I thought. *He spoke up to let me keep doing my thing because he saw I was making big plays. I want to prove him right.*

That was a moment I carried with me through not only the rest of that game but throughout my standout sophomore season. *Aaron Donald noticed me and advocated for me. I want to do what he believed I could.*

A few years later, when he was a Pro Bowler and top-ranked player for the Rams, Aaron was tapped to present the ACC's Brian Piccolo Award, which honors "the most courageous player in the conference." In case you hadn't already guessed, the award is named in honor of Brian Piccolo, a fullback out of Wake Forest who was named ACC Player of the Year in 1964 and went on to start for the Chicago Bears before dying from cancer at age twenty-six. I'd seen the classic movie *Brian's Song*, based on his story, and I was deeply moved to have been selected for the honor in light of the incredible legacy Piccolo left. But it became even more special when Aaron Donald, one of my role models, announced to a packed room, "I'm James's number one fan." He was proud that I was carrying on the legacy he had helped create at our alma mater. He encouraged me when I was a young guy, just starting to make a name for myself, and he encouraged me again when he could see I was facing something even bigger than trying to build a football career. He saw my potential, and his encouragement made me want to rise to the occasion—to do even more and make my best even better. *If one person's encouragement can inspire so much*, I thought, *what can a lot of encouragement do—and how can I find opportunities to encourage people more in the future?*

In fact, the more I looked around, the more I was amazed by the grassroots support I encountered at every turn during my battle with cancer. It seemed like I had support coming at me from a dozen different directions and from as diverse and surprising a collection of people as I could imagine.

The day after my initial press conference to announce my diagnosis, Ryan Switzer, a University of North Carolina football player I had gotten to know at football camps when we were both in high school, wrote #ConnerStrong on his cleats for the ACC Championship Game against Clemson. That was my first hint that my story might resonate beyond just my own town. A week or two later, my grandmama called to let me know that her preacher did a piece on me in his sermon that week. "Sweetheart," she said, "we had the whole church praying for you." That's when I knew it was resonating outside the college football world, too.

Then Eric Berry reached out from Kansas City, and I benefited greatly from our communication. "When I was first diagnosed, someone reached out to me," he said, "so I'm just paying it forward." I realized my story had reached the NFL. Sure enough, not long after that, Dan Quinn, the head coach of the Atlanta Falcons, sent me a card to let me know he was thinking of me. I have no idea how he first heard my story, but his gesture not only showed me my story was still spreading and touching people but also reminded me I wasn't invisible to the NFL, after all. That gave me a little more hope for rebuilding my career the following year.

Then, in April, when former president Bill Clinton spoke on the Pitt campus, Jesse Irwin, the host of a campus radio show called

Pitt Tonight, had a chance to talk with him and asked him to sign a get-well card for me. "James," the president wrote, "hang in there—it's a contest you can win!" That happened around the same time as my appearance on *Ellen*, and combined with the support I received after that episode aired, I realized my story resonated well beyond just the sports world.

I was stunned. Humbled. Amazed. Inspired. I couldn't believe that so many people I didn't even know would take it upon themselves to support me. My high school coaches reached out to me, too. That's when Coach Soboleski reminded me of something. "You've *always* had a huge team on your side," he explained. "When you were in high school, you made sure to get to know everyone's name—not just your teammates, coaches, and trainers, but the maintenance people and cafeteria workers. You were friends with everyone from the shiest kid in class to the most popular kid in school."

"But why would so many people step up now?" I asked.

"Because you made it a goal to have real, personal interactions with as many people as you could. You made everyone feel like they had a place in our school," he said. "Now, I think people want to encourage you in the same way."

His words surprised me: I had always thought of myself as a pretty quiet guy and definitely not a very emotive person. Outside of my group of close friends and teammates, I wasn't especially outgoing. I mean, I tried to be friendly with all the people I encountered, but I didn't think I made much of an impact on them. My parents raised me to treat everyone with respect; in fact, one of my stepdad's favorite pieces of advice was "Be nice to everybody. Don't talk bad about anyone." He reminded us of that before we left for school in the morning when we were kids, and he'd say it again if we started complaining about someone in class or on our team. I took those words to heart. They were so simple, yet so powerful.

In fact, in the midst of everything, I received a Facebook message from a teammate I knew in high school. He was a freshman when I was a junior, so I didn't know him that well, but he always stood out to me because he was a really hard worker even though he didn't get much playing time. This is what he wrote:

You might not remember me, but I played football with you and worked out with you and everyone called me "Big Sexy" or FB. It means "Fat Bastard," but you were the only one that called me by my name. My biggest was 398, almost 400 pounds.

You told me something that stuck with me through school. You said nobody can tell you what you want but you. And I wanted to lose weight. It took about 3 years, but I'm down to 175 lbs, and I wanted to say thank you for helping me think about what I wanted.

I couldn't believe it. Someone whose work ethic I genuinely admired and who I wanted to support not only took my words to heart but recognized his own strength and potential to change his own life. I was so honored to have played some small part in his journey toward health and happiness. That message reminded me of the importance of kindness—and the power of words. We can tear each other down or build each other up using the exact same tools; I'd rather be a builder. I'd rather be someone who cheers other people on and encourages them on their own journeys than someone who tries to derail them.

It doesn't take much to impact a person's whole day, which can help change the trajectory of their whole life. I've always tried to have meaningful interactions with people—to actually learn their names and what they care about—but I never really thought of those things as particularly encouraging. But after thinking about what my high school coach told me, I realized that maybe that's exactly what encouragement is: brief but meaningful interactions that have a positive outcome. I didn't set out to encourage people individually, but I somehow managed it simply by living out the values my parents instilled in me from a young age.

It turns out that all we have to do to encourage others is simply acknowledge them—make them feel seen and heard. Make them feel they matter. Really, that's all anyone wants—to be reminded that they matter to someone. Encouragement doesn't require a massive investment. It doesn't mean you have to break yourself to lift someone else up. It's just injecting a little extra positivity into the world and hoping someone benefits from it.

The same is true in reverse, too. It's possible to draw encouragement just from watching *someone else* do something uplifting— seeing a stranger pause for a few minutes to speak with a homeless person instead of just passing by, watching someone offer a smile and a "Hang in there!" to the frazzled parent with a crying toddler at the grocery store, overhearing another passenger on the plane speak kindly to the overworked attendant on a delayed flight. Even if the action or intention isn't directed toward you, you can still find yourself strengthened and empowered by witnessing a moment of goodness. When something simple but beautiful unfolds before your eyes, you realize that you are capable of doing those same things. What encouragement creates above and beyond everything else is hope.

In fact, encouragement is so important that in the book of Romans, Paul even lists it as a "spiritual gift," one of the important characteristics that believers can use to help spread the love of God. In 1 Corinthians, he writes, "And now these three remain: faith, hope and love. But the greatest of these is love." And what is love, exactly? It's showing compassion. It's extending a hand. It's meeting needs. It's affirming the worth of an individual. Encouragement is a form of love.

My grandmama definitely understands the connection between the three, and she ties them all together perfectly. As a kid, the emotion I associated most with her was laughter. Whenever we got together for family gatherings, the kids would play downstairs and the adults would sit and talk upstairs. Us kids used to wonder if the floor was going to cave in from all the foot-stomping we heard from the adults upstairs as Grandmama cracked everyone up. She is someone who radiates joy. Even when she told us stories about living in North Carolina in the civil rights era—having to buy a "colored bus pass" or drink from a separate water fountain—she didn't let bitterness creep into her voice. She kept her eyes focused on the beauty of the world and encouraged her family to rise above any brokenness, ugliness, or judgment. When I was a kid, she loved to offer practical advice: "Be small with money, and don't owe anyone anything," she would remind us. It never felt like she was lecturing or scolding us because everything she said was so rooted in love. You could hear the faith in her voice and the pleasure she took in offering you bits of wisdom and perspective to help you build your own best path forward. When I talked to her, I was always filled with hope that the future was going to be beautiful.

Nothing changed after my diagnosis; if anything, Grandmama got even more encouraging. She pulled out all her prayer guns, texting me her prayers for me each day and sharing prayers I could say if I was struggling to come up with the words to express what I felt.

I began to take screenshots of her messages so that I could pull them up and refer back to them at times when I needed to remember that I had people on their knees for me. Even now that I'm in the pros, she texts me before games, saying, "Remember your grandma is praying for you." I can't think of a greater gift than the knowledge that she is lifting me up to God so regularly. Faith, hope, and love—that's Grandmama in three words. She is the embodiment of encouragement, and I hope I can be even half as good at it as she is.

Encouragement matters. The way we reach out to other people keeps us connected to one another. To know that someone cares enough to remember you in the midst of their own busyness is a beautiful and humbling thing. When we offer encouragement, we give people the power to keep persevering, we make people feel less alone, we remind people of their inherent value, and we build community. These are all things the world could use more of right now.

All the people I loved, and so many more I didn't even know, united to keep me strong during treatment and keep my dreams alive for the future. That hope was what kept me going—their encouragement allowed me to have faith that better days lie ahead. Without that motivation, there would have been no reason to keep fighting.

Encouragement is the food of hope. It is what nourishes the belief that things will work out, that circumstances can change, that difficult times won't last forever, and that something better is coming. It is what helps someone face the next opponent or even just take the next breath or the next step. When all your fight is gone and all your strength is drained, sometimes the only thing that can give you the courage to keep going is someone on the sideline shouting, "You've got this!" or someone in your ear whispering, "I believe in you."

What may take you ten seconds to type and send might change the whole course of a person's day. A postage stamp might mean nothing to you, but that card might be the thing that gives someone the strength to face another day. One kind word that costs you nothing could completely alter the way a person sees their situation. It doesn't matter what you do; encouragement is about the gesture. It's the ultimate embodiment of "It's the thought that counts." Often, people shy away from reaching out because they don't know what to say or they are afraid of accidentally saying the wrong thing. That is totally understandable; when in doubt, I just say less. A card that simply states "I am thinking of you during this difficult time" or a text that reads "How are you?" or "Checking in" communicates exactly as much as flowery prose would.

Whether you write notes, offer high fives, pray, or bake cookies, offering encouragement is a way to remind other people and ourselves that we are all connected in this world. It may look like something simple, but it feels a lot like love.

CHAPTER 10

YOU ARE NOT YOUR OBSTACLE

On May 9, 2016, I went to Hillman for my final chemo treatment. In the two weeks leading up to it, I struggled through final exams and end-of-course projects. But that was nothing compared to the two weeks that followed, constantly worrying and wondering if my chemo really was behind me or if I would have to endure another round or undergo surgery. As you might imagine, there was a whole lot of praying going on.

Fourteen days later, on the morning of May 23, I woke up early before my final screening at the hospital to determine whether or not the cancer was still in my system. A bundle of nerves, I decided to read my daily devotional before Mom and I left to meet Mr. Gallagher and Meghan, who were coming along to the appointment as moral support. I was reading *Jesus Calling* by Sarah Young at the time, which has since become one of my favorite devotionals, and the thought for the day included these lines: "Before you get out of bed, I have already been working to prepare the path that will get you through this day. There are hidden treasures strategically placed along the way. Some of the treasures are trials, designed to shake you from earth-shackles. Others are blessings that reveal My Presence: sunshine, flowers, birds, friendships, answered prayers."

As soon as I read that, all the worry I had been carrying melted away. Everything was in God's hands, whether I released it to Him or not. I could either continue to fret about the things that were beyond my control or I could step into the day feeling peace and assurance that everything would happen according to God's plan, no matter what the tests showed.

I felt calm sitting in the hospital, waiting for the chest X-ray, PET scan, and blood draw. I knew that I had an identity beyond the label cancer stamped on me; I was a child of God. No diagnosis could trump that or change it. Just because I was calm didn't mean I wasn't eager for results, though. As I soon as I changed out of the hospital gown after the scan, I called Dr. Marks's cell phone. "What does the scan show?" I asked him.

"James," he said, patiently, "I haven't even had a chance to download the images yet. I promise I will call you as soon as we have the results." Mom, Mr. Gallagher, Meghan, and I loaded into the car and headed back toward Pitt's football practice facility on the south side of town. My phone rang just a few minutes later as we drove down Centre Avenue. It was Dr. Marks.

Mr. Gallagher quickly pulled over so he could film the conversation, since he had been so committed to documenting the whole cancer journey for me. As I sat in the backseat and listened to Dr. Marks go over all my results, I started crying at the words I had been waiting to hear for the past five months, two weeks, and six days: "There's no sign of cancer."

I put my hand to my eyes as the tears fell; everyone in the car cheered. "The Cheesecake Factory is just over the bridge," someone— I think it was my mom—said. "We need to go celebrate." As we walked inside the restaurant a few minutes later, I furiously typed the news into the Twitter app on my phone:

God is AMAZING. Just got the call that my body is clean of cancer!!! Been a long road but God had my back. Thanks everyone who said prayers.

We enjoyed a celebratory lunch with a lot—a *lot*—of food; Cheese- cake Factory was one of the places I had stopped eating at during my treatment so it didn't get ruined for me, so I was making up for lost time. Then Mom and the Gallaghers dropped me off at the Duratz Athletic Complex, which players just called "the facility," right as practice was wrapping up. Everyone checks their phones first thing, as soon as the final whistle blows—sometimes even before grabbing water—so word was already out before I even got there. Everyone started clapping and congratulating me as soon as I walked in. I had beaten cancer. God had answered the thousands and thousands of prayers in the way we'd hoped. Later that afternoon, my good news would even appear on the scrolling news feed in Times Square, but at that moment, all I cared about was that my teammates—the guys who had been by my side the past three years and especially the past six months—were celebrating with me.

"Number twenty-four is BACK!" I grinned. That was it. I was

back to being just good old #24 again—not the sick guy, not the guy working out in the mask. Cancer had not won. It did not have any more power over my life. It did not get to determine my future. I was cancer-free.

The moment you receive life-changing news, it's all you can think about—trust me. It's the first thing on your mind when you get up in the morning and the last thing running through your head before you fall asleep. When you are hanging out with your friends, you're still aware that your body is actively waging battle. When you're trying to focus on class, work, or practice, your brain is still turning over the reality that what you're facing is truly life-or-death.

I've talked to a lot of other cancer patients who have had the same experience. Even when it seems like you might be enjoying yourself doing something else, the diagnosis is still there like a new body part that is with you wherever you go. What might have once just been a sore throat, a small bruise, or an annoying headache now has you researching symptoms and worrying about complications. The diagnosis never leaves you.

Because the diagnosis leads to such a complete transformation of how you view everything, it can also greatly affect your sense of identity. It's one thing to research your condition and read up on treatment options; it's another thing to rely on it to explain other parts of your life: *My future looks like _____ because of my prognosis.* And, just like that, you've turned your health status into a horoscope and your diagnosis into your destiny.

I'm sure the same is true for any kind of major life upheaval. Obviously, my experience is with a serious medical issue, but that doesn't mean that these same lessons don't apply to a thousand other labels someone might slap on you based on your own obstacles. It could be that your brain is wired to learn differently or interact with other people in an atypical way. It could even be something in your past that is holding you back.

The thing to remember, no matter what you are facing, is this: You are *not* your circumstances. It doesn't matter what your obstacles are—a medical diagnosis, challenges with your mental or emotional health, difficulties learning, a rough childhood, or bad decisions in your past—you are not defined by the labels others have put on you. Just because something makes you "different" from whatever normal is supposed to look like doesn't mean that challenge has to be your defining feature. You need to know that. You are *not* your obstacles. Not even close.

You may be asking, "But, James, what does it *really* matter whether or not you allow your challenge to become your identity?" It actually matters a lot, because your identity can easily become your destiny. If your vision of yourself is that "I am sick, so I can't do/be/accomplish/hope for _____," you are handing the reins of power over to your obstacle. Don't surrender that easily. You are the one who gets to call the shots on what influences your future.

An obstacle also doesn't mean your life has to come to a screeching halt. Limitations don't mean you stop living. I definitely understand that many illnesses and intense treatments can leave you feeling physically exhausted. I also understand the challenges of feeling your body grow weaker. Things will be different; that can't be denied. And we all know that there are some conditions that simply don't have a cure. But life inevitably ends in death for all of us. It's something everyone will have to face sooner or later. I know that sounds bleak, but it doesn't have to be. The real question is what are you going to do with the time between now and then? Sure, you may feel fatigued more easily, but a little extra sleep doesn't equal surrender. A diagnosis—no matter how devastating—is not a death sentence. It's how much time you have left to live. Don't be defeated until you actually are.

Looking around Hillman on my treatment days, I noticed three main types of people: those who were positive and energetic, those who were tired but still seemed to find joy in life, and those whose cancer hung over them like a black cloud. I could empathize with every group. I tried to be positive and energetic on most days, but there were some times when I simply didn't have it in me to do anything more than shut my eyes and power through the next treatment. The emotional weight of the disease is like watching your life in fast-forward and mourning all the things you'll miss—all the little moments that make up day-to-day living and all the big, momentous events that become family lore. You miss the times when your biggest worries were so much smaller, and you grieve the things you don't want to miss. It's a complicated, exhausting, confusing jumble of emotions.

Once you get earth-shattering news like a cancer diagnosis, it's impossible to shake it off, even on the best days. I'm definitely not trying to shame anyone for how they respond to something life-changing. But I also know that I didn't want cancer to have any more power over me than it already did, which meant that I was going to continue to live as fully as I could for as long as I could. An obstacle is no reason to hit pause on your life.

It is important to remember that moving forward can often look like a big question mark, at least until you are back in the normal rhythm of life. There are new routines, new habits, new roles established during a crisis, and it might take a little while to get things back to normal. The longer-term future often is a little different or a little murkier for people facing particularly challenging experiences, too. Remember what I said about the diagnosis always being present? Even after you get the "all clear" from your doctor, there's still a whisper in the back of your mind saying, "But what if it comes back?" If I wake up sweaty one morning, I have to ask myself, "Was this an AC issue or lymphoma night sweats?" Those questions will probably never totally leave me. It's up to us to either live in the shadow of what we've endured or redefine ourselves on *our* terms.

We all face challenges in our everyday lives, and I'm by no means trying to discount these very real difficulties. What I *am* saying is that the exercise I found to be the most helpful was finding the mental space where I could accept that I was facing something serious, but where I could also set down the worry and not be controlled by it.

It's a tricky balance. We want people to be mindful of the battle we're fighting, but we also don't want them to treat us like we're made of glass. Because my immune system was so weakened during treatment and I had to wear a mask, I felt like I was a walking billboard advertising: "I'm sick!" I struggled with feeling so conspicuous about something I was trying to play down. At the same time, I felt incredibly free the first time I walked into the gym for conditioning and nobody made a big deal about it. Everyone treated me exactly the same as they always had. I was just another guy working out with my team. That was all I ever wanted to be.

In anticipation of our morning practices, I set my alarm for 4:00 a.m. every day, which gave me exactly enough time to get dressed, brush my teeth, make a bowl of oatmeal, and walk to the bus stop to catch the 4:15 bus. It was a ten-minute ride to the workout facility, so I was on the field well ahead of our start time of 4:45. I worried that the first time I gave in to the temptation to hit the snooze button with the rationale that "I'm fighting cancer, I deserve to sleep in," I would give into that same temptation the day after that, too. I never wanted to let that kind of excuse-based thinking color my outlook. If I wanted to be a football player, then I had to treat myself like a football player, not a cancer patient. That had to be the lens through which I viewed everything else. I was still a leader, which meant that my example still mattered, even if I wasn't on the field with the rest of my team. My obstacle was not going to control my life; my commitment to my team and my dreams, however, was another story.

I could have slept through morning practice and no one would have batted an eye. But I was determined to be there for practice, no matter what, and my teammates responded accordingly. They never made me feel different or pitied or broken—they made me feel like myself again. They encouraged me and cheered me on, but it never seemed as if they were afraid of me or afraid *for* me when we were all together. My cancer did not take on a life of its own because of them. It did not become another teammate to whom we all deferred. That didn't mean that we pretended nothing was wrong; it just meant that when my friends looked at me, they still saw *me* first and foremost, not my obstacle.

Waiting in line for the bench press bar in the weight room, we still joked around with each other. Cheering one another on, we each took a turn trying to set a personal record—myself included. Wiping sweat off my face with my shirt, I focused on how much better

I had done than the day before. I didn't want to think about where my numbers were just a few months ago or the fact that everything felt hotter breathing through a surgical mask. I was committed to focusing on the present moment, doing what I loved, surrounded by a team that still respected and encouraged me—nothing more, nothing less.

After all, nothing had changed about my practice philosophy, my drive, or my sense of competition. Going easy on myself would have meant that I was letting cancer win; I had no intention of giving up. Spending part of every day with my team—with people who made me happy and who pushed me to do better—was an essential part of my recovery. Time with friends who understood that and made me feel like myself again was one of the most important things that allowed me to move forward in faith rather than become paralyzed by fear.

My childhood friend Carson helped me find the balance better than just about anyone else. Whenever I went back to Erie for a weekend, he was always available to hang out, get food, or just sit and talk for as long as a I needed. He always waited for me to bring up the cancer; he never forced the topic. Sometimes I wanted to talk about it, sometimes I didn't. He always asked how I was doing and checked in with me in between visits, but he never tried to reduce our time together to just a discussion about my health.

When I was home in Erie over spring break, I remarked to Carson that I was tired of feeling so hemmed in by all the restrictions on what I could do and where I could go. He shrugged. "Want to go hoop?"

Fifteen minutes later, we were at the open gym at Our Lady of Peace School, playing five-on-five basketball with some of Carson's cousins and friends. At first, the guys looked at Carson as if to ask, "Is James actually playing right now?" Then he checked me the ball and we started running down the court. One of my teammates from Pitt, Qadree Ollison, was staying the week with me, and he just laughed at the concerns that I shouldn't be hitting the court. He had seen me at practice every day, so he knew I wasn't in any kind of delicate condition.

I took off my mask and threw myself into the game. It felt good to do something normal again; I needed that time away from my sickness, my treatments, and all the stress that went along with them. We played ball for several hours—until they turned off the lights, in fact. "That was awesome," I told Carson as we drove back to his house. "I got to just be me again."

Carson could have insisted we stay in his basement and play Xbox or he could have tried to go easy on me on the court, but he just treated me like he always had. He respected that I was more than my disease, my treatment, or my fight. Those things were a huge part of my life at the moment, of course, but he helped me remember that they didn't define me.

Well-meaning people often fall back on these generalizations because they are so easy. People are naturally associative; we draw connections between things as a way of classifying, ordering, and ultimately understanding the world around us. When you receive a serious diagnosis, you take on a new identity to a lot of people. You become "the kid with type 1 diabetes" or "the woman who learned in college that she had multiple sclerosis" or "the guy who got cancer." It's not that anyone is trying to narrow your significance down to one single thing; it's that they are trying to make sense of your experience the same way. Your challenge is what makes you unique to them, but it can feel limiting, simplistic, and even dehumanizing—which is especially frustrating when you want to be known for other reasons. You may have a challenge, but that doesn't mean you become a whole new person. This issue can also be a challenge for caregivers, family, and friends of someone going through a difficult time. If you find yourself in that role, you might struggle with how to acknowledge your loved one's experience without reducing them to their condition. It's tempting to want to send someone every article you read about alternative treatment options or celebrities who share their condition. You may even struggle with how to relate to them and worry about tiptoeing around triggering topics; a serious diagnosis can be a kind of trauma, after all. That's a lot of pressure, and you feel it because you love that person and you want them to know that you are on this journey with them. That's a beautiful thing, and I want to applaud you for it.

It is a tricky area to navigate, though, and I encourage you to take your lead from the person experiencing the challenge. If they seem open to talking about their condition or exploring other treatments, then go ahead and share—but also be prepared to stop if they don't respond positively. And if they don't seem to want to talk about it, don't force the issue. If they don't show an interest in discussing alternative treatments, trust people to know their own boundaries. Two things to remember: first, the person going through the obstacle has almost certainly done more research on it than you have; and second, they don't owe you any information about their prognosis, treatment, emotional state, outside assistance, or anything else that is helping them get through this difficult time. I don't mean that to sound harsh, but I do think it is important to remember that no matter how public someone's battle may seem, it's still their right to maintain their privacy.

I think most people who are going through a major struggle feel the same way. It's nice to be mindful of their situation and accepting of their limitations, but don't treat them like a different person. You can make someone feel respected without making them feel weak. You can honor their experience without wallowing in it. Cancer didn't kill my sense of humor or my sense of competition—if anything, it made them both stronger. I didn't want people to think they had to be serious around me just because I was going through something serious, and laughter is a better alternative to crying 99 percent of the time.

One other word of advice to friends and family: through my own serious health struggle, I've found that it can be really helpful to mark my calendar with significant dates for loved ones going through their own difficult times. People are great at reaching out when your diagnosis is fresh news, but it can sometimes get lonely weeks or months or even years into the struggle. Maybe you can make a note to text the person each year on the anniversary of their diagnosis—trust me, they remember the significance of the date even if no one else does. If you are afraid of overstepping, you don't have to say anything more than "I just wanted you to know I always think of you this time of year. I hope you are doing well." It lets someone know you haven't forgotten what they went through, that you recognize that their battle was a major event in their life, and that it does not have to be their controlling narrative going forward.

When September 3, 2016, finally rolled around and I laced those beautiful cleats onto my feet ahead of our season opener against Villanova, I felt like a new man. Actually, scratch that—I felt like my old self again, which I hadn't felt in almost a year. I was physically and mentally strong, and I was itching to be back in the game after twelve months on the sidelines. I knew the cancer was going to be on everyone's mind: Was I ready to be back on the field? Could I still play? Could my body handle hard runs and harder hits? I knew the sportscasters on TV were going to be talking about my story every time I made a play, but I couldn't control that. All I could do was play my best game and trust my teammates to treat me as they would anyone else on our team. And they did.

In the second quarter, I got the handoff from our quarterback, Nathan Peterman, and took off three yards toward the end zone. The last yard or so I stiff-armed the guy chasing me as I pushed my way over the line to score the first touchdown of the game. There was a moment as I picked myself up off the ground that time stood still as my brain registered the magnitude of what just happened: *I can't believe I'm back to doing what I love.* Then my teammates swarmed me and I was back in the middle of the game, just a guy who had managed to make a big play. A few drives later, with nineteen seconds left in the half, I sprinted down the field as Peterman lobbed a perfect nine-yard pass right to my outstretched hands. I grabbed the ball and pulled it to my chest as three Villanova defenders slammed into me, but I hit the ground on the right side of the line and hung six more points on the board. Here it was, my first game back, and I managed to score the first two touchdowns. It was like Dev Edwards had reminded me over and over, God was the one writing my story—and He made that first game back even better than I could have imagined.

In November 2018, nine-year-old Joey visited Heinz Field as part of a Make-A-Wish Foundation wish grant. Joey had recently completed his last cancer treatment, which meant he was finally healthy enough to come to a Steelers game. Our staff whisked Joey all around the facility, introducing him to a variety of people. When I finally had a chance to visit with Joey one-on-one, he greeted me with a huge smile and announced, "I had cancer, too!" We had a good time swapping stories and just talking about life in general. I gave him my game gloves and congratulated him on being a survivor, but there was one other message I wanted to make sure he heard above everything else. "Your cancer is behind you," I said, looking him squarely in the eye. "Now is the time to live and enjoy life."

For the rest of his life, Joey will be a "cancer survivor." That is a title he earned and should wear proudly. But it is not the heart of his identity or mine or anyone else's who's had cancer. We have an entire life ahead of us that *cancer hasn't touched*. Our life going forward is totally uncharted territory, and no one gets to call the shots as to what shape it takes except for us. We can't choose exactly what our future will look like, but we get to determine the meaning and significance it brings to ourselves and to the world.

The same is true for anyone who is facing a challenge. Don't let your obstacle color your dreams. By all means, be a survivor! But also be a friend, an avid reader, an athlete, a football fan, an Eagle Scout, a teacher, an artist—and whatever else you'd like to be, too. You aren't locked into one path simply because of the hand life dealt you. A challenge is not a sentence handed down to determine the rest of your life; it's simply the obstacle you have to deal with in this particular season of your life. It may have lingering effects or lasting repercussions, but it is not the be-all and end-all of who you are. You are more than simply what happened to you; your real identity lies in what you *choose* to do with the life you've got.

Whatever challenge you are facing, remember that you are more than your obstacles and more than your fears. You are not your setback or your employment status or whether or not you are in a relationship or your trauma or whatever else you might be battling at the moment. Those things may be happening to you, but they are not *who* you are. If this is where you are right now—facing obstacles that make you question your sense of self and your place in the world—allow yourself to experience your unique path, but don't for a second believe your challenge is the most important thing about you. Your obstacles don't determine your worth or your future. Your worth comes from the fact that you are created by a God who has very specific plans for you, and your future is determined by your choices, not your circumstances.

Let your identity be shaped by what you stand for and how you pursue your passions. Be someone who is determined, courageous, kind, and joyful. Make the decision each day to be someone who does things—things that matter, things that bring joy, things that are life-giving to you and others—rather than just being someone to whom something happened. Root your identity in the positive. No matter how intimidating the problem, it can't define you unless you let it. Don't ever let it.

CHAPTER 11

EMBRACE YOUR STORY

If you went looking for me at 11:00 p.m. on Friday, April 28, 2017, you would have found me sitting in a chair at Buffalo Wild Wings in Erie, Pennsylvania, staring stoically at a giant screen for the second night in a row. It may not sound like a particularly stressful situation, but it was one of the most nerve-racking nights I've ever experienced.

After six months of chemotherapy and finally getting the all clear on my health the previous May, the fall at Pitt had been punctuated by a series of great games. I broke a couple of school and conference records, which shut down most speculation that my body had been through too much to ever play at an elite level again. It was a good enough season that, on December 10, 2016 (a full month *before* the deadline to apply and 375 days *after* my cancer diagnosis), I announced my intention to forgo my final year at Pitt and enter the NFL draft. I had traded my fear for patience over the past year while I waited and worked; now, the wait was almost over. Even though it came a season later than I had planned for, I knew it was finally time for me to step into my professional dream.

Thursday, April 27, 2017, was the first night of the draft, and my hometown buzzed with excitement to see who would pick me. A local news crew came to Buffalo Wild Wings to film me while I watched the draft selections and waited for my phone to ring. Friends, family, fans, and even my high school coach, Mark Soboleski, all came out to support me. I could feel the love in the room as we all watched the big TV screen to watch the picks start to shake out, and we held our breath, hoping for the call that would change my life and make all the hard work worth it.

The draft kicked off and two running backs—guys whose highlight reels I'd studied in my chemo chair—were selected in the top ten, but they were the only two running backs to go in the first round. I tried not to glance at my phone too compulsively as the evening wore on. Four nerve-racking hours later, when the first round wrapped up and I wasn't selected, we were all a little disappointed but not disheartened. Life doesn't always follow the script you'd like it to, as I well understood by that point. There is something magical about going in the first round, and we all hoped for the fairy-tale ending to my dramatic college career, but there were still six more rounds to go, which would take place over the following two days. When I walked into Buffalo Wild Wings the next evening at 7:00 p.m. for James's NFL Draft Watch Party—Part II, I was ready to take the second round by storm.

Like the night before, only two running backs were picked in the second round—and neither one was me. My marketing manager, Nima Zarrabi, was at the party. Nima and my agent, Ryan Tollner from Rep 1 Sports, were the guys who stayed with me when every other agency that had been courting me during my record-breaking sophomore year suddenly went silent the second I announced my diagnosis. Nima runs on coffee, loyalty, and hustle, and he was fueled by all three that night, checking his phone, stepping out to make calls, stepping back in to let me know the teams that were looking at me and what upcoming picks might go my way. But those picks went by and my phone didn't ring. My name wasn't announced. My pride suffered a little more with each possibility that didn't come through.

I was confident I would go in the second round, but now, three hours in, the third round began. Surely I'd go at the top of the third, but my phone stayed stubbornly silent as it rested on my knee. I stared at it, willing it to ring. In my head, I listed all the deep-pick selections who had gone on to have impressive careers: Russell Wilson had gone in the third round; Darren Sproles didn't get selected until the fourth; Kurt Warner went undrafted and so did Warren Moon. Come to think of it, Brian Piccolo had been the ACC Player of the Year in 1964, and he went undrafted before becoming a starter for the Bears. Ultimately, where I was picked didn't matter nearly as much as what I actually achieved for the team, right? But which team was actually going to give me a shot?

As the third round wore on, the mood in the room grew more muted. I was emotionless, stung by each team that passed over me, trying to ignore the knots in my stomach, and doing my best not to show all the questions running through my head: *How different would this have been if I'd never torn my MCL? What if I'd been able to play my junior year? How much of this is being influenced by my cancer?* I knew that my story wasn't a typical one and that some teams might be unsure about what lay ahead for my health and career in the future. I had hoped that they would be able to look past my challenges and focus on my statistics—my on-field performance spoke for itself. But as teams continued to make their picks without calling my name, I couldn't help but feel like I was being penalized or singled out because I'd had cancer and because it could come back. *Fear is a choice!* I wanted to tell the coaches. *You can choose to be afraid of what might happen with my health or you can give me a chance to prove how dedicated I am, how I break down every obstacle that stands in my way.* The night wore on, and I still didn't have a team.

When Jonnu Smith went to the Tennessee Titans as the one hundredth pick, my brain turned into a complete pessimist. *That's it; we're in triple digits now,* I thought. My shoulders dropped and my chest sank. *You're not going tonight. You're going to slide to the fourth round.*

At that exact moment, Nima came back inside, tapped me on the shoulder, and leaned in. "You're going to be getting a call soon," he whispered. "Don't answer your phone unless it is a 412 area code." I just stared at him like he was crazy. I wasn't skipping any phone calls; I didn't care what area code the call came from as long as there was a head coach on the other line.

Just as Denver announced their selection of Brendan Langley—101st overall—my phone rang. Everyone froze as I answered, putting my finger in my ear so I could actually make out the voice on the other end while the draft coverage blared on in the background.

"James? Mike Tomlin, Pittsburgh Steelers."

My heart stopped as I heard the head coach's voice, but I tried not to freak out. "What's up, Coach? What's going on?"

"Where are you at?" he asked. "Are you in Erie?"

"Yes, sir," I answered. "I'm up here in Erie."

"Well, we're not going to reimburse you for your gas mileage," he laughed, "but we are interested in making you a Pittsburgh Steeler."

"Coach, I don't need the gas money."

He laughed again. "Well, I'm excited for you and your family."

I struggled to stay calm as we went over some administrative details with a few other folks he had had hop onto the call.

"My wife knows all about your story and she is so happy we selected you, she's crying," Steelers general manager Kevin Colbert told me. I understood how she felt; I was about to start crying myself.

Still on the phone, I stood up and walked toward where my brothers were sitting with my dad. They couldn't hear what I was saying, but they knew what this call was about, and they all hugged me.

As we wrapped up, Coach Tomlin got back on the line and said, "James, I haven't been this excited about a draft pick in a long time."

"Thank you, Coach. I won't let you down," I assured him. Then I pressed the red button, looked at my family, all born and raised in western Pennsylvania, deeply rooted in these hills and rivers—just like me. Trying to stay calm, I couldn't stop my eyes from crinkling up with joy as I quietly said, "I'm staying home."

I didn't say another word as I went back to my chair and laced my fingers together over my head, but my hands kept slipping off because I was sweating so badly. My mom and grandma each grabbed an arm and leaned into my shoulders. I closed my eyes, took a few deep, steadying breaths, and waited. I wouldn't let myself believe it completely until I heard Arthur Moats at the podium. A few minutes later, and with a huge smile that spilled over to his voice, he leaned into the microphone and announced: "Now, with the

105th pick in the 2017 NFL draft, the Pittsburgh Steelers select . . . James Conner—running back, Pittsburgh."

The restaurant erupted. I kept my eyes closed for a moment, then dropped my head in relief. Even when I eventually stood up, I still kept my head down. *Thank you, Lord,* I repeated in my head. *You are the One who brought me to this moment. Thank you. Thank you.* All this time, I had been worried that my story was keeping teams away, but my hometown team—the people who knew my story better than anyone—were the ones who said, "We want YOU."

When a reporter asked how I was feeling, I struggled to control the emotion in my voice: "It's an unbelievable feeling, man. I'm going right back to Heinz Field."

"Did you see this happening a year ago or two years ago?" the reporter pressed.

"I knew I was going to be in the NFL one day," I said. "Everything I've been through was just a bump in the road. But I'm thankful for it all."

That bump in the road—my cancer diagnosis—felt like a mountain at times, but it was never insurmountable. I preferred to view it as a speedbump that never knocked me off course, but it did force me to take my foot off the gas for a minute. My battle with cancer forced me to slow down and made me look squarely at my experiences and face my story head-on.

I don't mean I struggled a little with what it all meant; I mean that I really had to wrestle with what my relationship was going to be with my cancer in the long run. How could I come to grips with this huge, life-changing event that drastically shifted the shape of my future? How should I deal with the speculation about my professional ambitions? I just wanted everything to go back to the way it was at the end of my sophomore season. I wanted the conversation to be about James Conner, the guy making big plays, not James Conner, the cancer survivor—who played some football, too.

At first, I really had a problem with the idea that cancer was always going to be associated with my name. Every discussion about me ahead of the draft seemed as focused on my diagnosis and recovery as it was on my time on the field. As much as I loved my experience on *Ellen,* I knew I hadn't been invited because I had broken some great record; I was there because I was the player fighting lymphoma. I wasn't sure what to do with my newfound fame—fame of a much different kind than I'd ever imagined. I suddenly became an "inspiration" simply because I fought to stay alive, just like anyone else in my shoes would have done. I didn't exactly feel like I deserved the attention.

All of these conflicting thoughts elbowed each other for space in my head as I started to prepare for life in the NFL. When it came time for me to select my Steelers jersey number, the number I'd worn in college was already taken, but #30—the same number I'd worn in high school—wasn't spoken for. That felt like the perfect nod to my hometown, to my roots, to my life before cancer.

Staying in western Pennsylvania was a dream come true, but it also brought a set of challenges I hadn't anticipated. Wherever I turned, it seemed like I was reminded of my past—especially the part I had fought so hard to leave behind. A few times, I met people who seemed surprised that I was gearing up to play professionally;

in their minds, I think I was always going to be the guy hooked up to the chemo drip.

I wanted people to let that part of my story go, but I knew it wasn't up to me. No matter what I accomplished on the field, whenever sportscasters talked about me, I knew my cancer story would be part of it. My identity is so much more than my cancer, and I wanted other people to see that, too. But I also knew I couldn't pretend like the cancer never happened; I couldn't erase that huge part of my journey. What I needed to find was a way to embrace my story without losing myself in it, and I decided that my best route was simply to give the commentators something else to talk about.

I threw myself into preseason training, determined to show up so ready to play that no one would even have a chance to think about my cancer. That had always worked for me before, after all. My philosophy was simple: be the hardest worker in the room and make that your identity. But there were two big problems with this plan. First, I was a rookie, and rookies rarely get much playing time in the NFL. Second, I was a rookie who was backing up one of the top running backs in the league. Here I was in the pros at last, and I was having flashbacks to high school—only this time, I couldn't just switch to defense. I believed in the importance of humility, keeping my head down, and waiting my turn. But it took a whole lot of self-control not to wonder if I would ever see much action on the field.

Come on, James, I lectured myself. *Haven't you learned anything about patience over the past year?*

You know how people always say talking to yourself isn't a problem, but answering yourself might be? Well, I had a problem, because the debates that raged in my head that spring were pretty intense.

Yes, I know I have to bide my time, but I also want to make up for lost time.

—Sure you do, but whose timing are you on—yours or God's?

God's, of course.

—Are you sure?

Well, I just want people to talk about something other than my cancer.

—Your MCL surgery?

Something other than that, too.

—Are you sure you're sure?

Why wouldn't I be?

I never really found a satisfactory answer, but I threw myself into our preseason training as if I were a starter. I was thrilled to be back at Heinz Field—truly my home field—and was excited to see how it looked on Sundays for Steelers games as opposed to Saturdays for Pitt games. Even though I knew I would be riding the bench for the foreseeable future, I was determined to turn the current conversation about "James Conner, the rookie who beat cancer," on its head.

The funny thing was, while I counted down the weeks to the preseason opener against the Giants on August 11, something completely unexpected was happening behind the scenes, and it was about to turn *my* plans upside down.

In the middle of July, I happened to run into my friend Sarah, who was still a cheerleader at Pitt. A friend of hers happened to work in the merchandising department for the Steelers, and she had the inside scoop. "I hear your jerseys are flying off the shelves," she said.

"Are you serious?" I asked. Considering I had yet to play a single down for the Steelers, I didn't have particularly high hopes for my jersey sales even breaking double digits. I mean, how many jerseys could my family wear at one time? That was about how many I had expected had sold at that point.

She nodded. "They were filling orders from Germany and Poland last week."

"Um . . . did you say *Poland*? Who in Poland even watches American football?"

"I don't know," she shrugged. "But someone does, apparently."

A few days later, I ran into someone else from the merchandising department in the cafeteria at Heinz Field. "James, have you heard about your jersey?" he asked as we carried our trays through the line.

"I heard it was doing pretty well," I said.

"We've had orders coming in from all over. Not just the U.S.—the world: Japan, Israel, Australia."

"Do they even have American football in Australia?"

"I'm not sure. But you've got fans there."

It didn't seem possible. The season hadn't even started, yet I was somehow already a fan favorite. Just a few days later, Dick's Sporting Goods tweeted that my jersey was the best-selling rookie jersey and closing in on Dak Prescott and Tom Brady for the top spot overall. Stories started to come in, too. People wrote to the Steelers organization to thank them for not being afraid of my diagnosis. People wrote to me to let me know they were excited that I was about to show the world what cancer survivors are capable of. The demographics for my jersey sales were surprising, too; a huge percentage of my orders were going to kids and women. Apparently, my

#30 was popular in breast cancer survivor groups because it represented a full life *after* the disease. The more I heard those stories and read the messages, the more it began to dawn on me that maybe I needed to rethink my perspective. My story was not something I needed to make everyone forget; it was something that could encourage people to remember that obstacles were made to be overcome. That dreams are worth chasing, even against the odds. That fear is a choice—and it's a choice we all have to make as we face the challenges life throws at us.

Despite making it my battle cry and even getting it tattooed on my forearm, I needed to be reminded that fear is a choice. For the past year, I had secretly harbored the fear that I was becoming famous for something that happened *to* me instead of something I had done. Now, I realized that I was looking at it all wrong. My story wasn't that I *had* cancer, but, rather, that I *fought* cancer. I pushed back. I kept working. I never lost sight of my dreams, trusting God to guide me forward. When I let go of my worry that my highlight reel might be turned into a recap of my health, I finally recognized that my story was *never* about what happened to me; it was about what I was going to *do* with what happened to me.

Finally, in the summer of 2017, I fully accepted the reality that had slowly dawned on me over the past year. As I started to see the impact my story had on people, I understood the importance of embracing the role I'd been given. After more than a year of trying to put it all behind me, I learned to embrace my story and, in doing so, I learned to love myself in a whole new way.

That might sound like a "fluff" response—self-love being at the heart of embracing our stories—but it's actually a key part of a pretty complex series of factors that led me to this shift in perspective. Over the year and a half from diagnosis to draft, I learned how deeply important it is to love yourself and your story—*your* story, not anyone else's. Your story is a huge part of your calling—the bigger purpose God has created specifically for you to impact the world.

It seems like we all want to be someone else or live a different life or enjoy a story that is different from the hand we've been dealt. Nearly everything in our society today is geared toward making us want something other than what we have. Advertisements show us beautiful people with luxurious clothes and jewelry. Social media influencers post pictures from gorgeous locations and amazing parties. Cultural pressures combine to remind us at every turn that someone has a life/house/body/job/story that is somehow inherently "better" than ours.

But you are you. You are in your position, living out your story for a reason. You were uniquely created to do something with the exact circumstances you're facing. Your story exists *for you*. Someone else's story exists for someone else. Don't wish yourself into someone else's life. Don't wish yourself out of your own story.

It took me a long time to really believe this. I could say that I was thankful for my cancer experience, like I told the reporter on the night I was drafted, but I knew that was what I was "supposed" to say. Being thankful was part of staying humble about how far I'd come, but I didn't actually understand yet what it meant to feel *truly* grateful for the experience the way I do now. I didn't grasp yet exactly how far-reaching my story was, or how much hope it gave to other people. I didn't understand yet that it's not about me at all, it's about what my story represents.

As I write this, I'm remembering the older gentleman I met yesterday who told me, with a cracking voice, how his adult son wears my jersey to his chemo treatments for courage. I'm recalling the tiny girl—no older than five or six—I met just a few weeks ago leaving an event at Heinz Field who hugged my leg and said I was her hero. I don't know her story—her dad just shook my hand and thanked me for all I do—but I doubt she cared where the Steelers ranked in the AFC North; to her, I represented life on the other side of the battle.

Though I was diagnosed in December 2015, I still meet people on a weekly basis who tell me my story encourages them. That is nothing I ever imagined when I received the diagnosis from my doctor and felt my future crumble in my hands. I didn't see any of this coming because I just wanted a clear, simple path. I only ever wanted to be a professional athlete—nothing more.

The moments when I meet people who have found meaning in my story remind me of the importance of owning what I've experienced. God used, and still uses, what I went through to connect me with some of the most amazing people on the planet. I've gotten to know entire communities of cancer survivors, lymphoma researchers, and health-care professionals I never would have met otherwise. I've talked with total strangers who have welcomed me into their lives because of my story. I have an entire life I never dreamed of because of the road I have traveled. Rejecting that part of my story would mean rejecting part of myself and rejecting the life that all of these incredible people helped to save, strengthen, and inspire.

In 2016, I received two awards that began to shift my thinking on this matter and allowed me to open my eyes to the real significance of what I had experienced. One was Disney's Sports Spirit Award, an annual honor given to college football's most inspiring individual or team. The second was the Courage Award from the Stanley M. Marks Blood Cancer Research Fund, named for the same Dr. Stanley Marks who oversaw my treatment and became like a family member to me in the process. That evening, to my complete surprise, the board announced that they had renamed it the James Conner Courage Award. These two honors were deeply humbling not only because of the prestige of the awards but because they started me on a path toward truly embracing my story. The awards weren't about my diagnosis; they were about my recovery and return to the game. As the name of each award suggested, they were about having spirit and courage; they were not about having cancer. Together, those awards opened the door that allowed me to recognize the incredible community my experiences now provided. My story is not about what happened to me, but what I did with it.

For most of my life, I tried in vain to live out my own vision for my future instead of embracing who God had called me to be. I wanted to find a place for God in *my* plans, rather than allowing God to place me where He wanted me in *His* plans. He gave me these experiences for a reason, and when I finally let go of my own stubborn idea of exactly the way things *should* be, I allowed God to strengthen me through my circumstances exactly as they were. Instead of changing my story, I needed to allow my story to change *me* for the better. As I looked back at everything God had led me through, I recognized that it was all part of the path He was clearing for me to do something significant with my experiences. And now was the time to step into the role He prepared for me all along. I had dreamed of playing in the NFL my whole life—but I wasn't dreaming big enough. God had so much more in store for me than becoming just a professional football player.

CHAPTER 12

PLAY FOR THOSE WHO CAN'T

Five-year-old Andrew O'Neil and I had a lot in common. He loved his big brother; I love my big brothers. He loved sports; I love sports. He was a huge Pitt fan; I was, too, obviously. He would go in for a chemo treatment and stay in the ICU overnight, then he would play in a baseball game twenty-four hours later. I understood how that felt, wrapping up chemo in the afternoon and hitting the practice field before dawn the next morning. Andrew was fighting neuroblastoma—a kind of nerve tissue cancer that, for him, resulted in a malignant tumor in his abdomen—but he pushed through the pain and nausea in order to be on the field, doing what he loved. He was my kind of guy. It didn't matter that Andrew was only five; I recognized that we were cut from the same cloth.

As soon as I learned about Andrew and his story, I couldn't wait to meet him. I finally had the chance in November 2016, when he was a guest at the Pitt game against Duke. As I walked toward Andrew and his family on the sidelines, the little boy's face lit up so brightly that I didn't even notice the tube running from his nose to where it disappeared in his shirt, or his bald head under his knit beanie, until after I'd been talking to him for a while. It was November, and he was bundled up in gold and blue, our team colors, but he was on fire for football and for life! His smile was absolutely electric, and his eyes took everything in. It was obvious that he had a zest for life that no amount of pain or sickness could steal from him. He gave me a huge hug and we talked for a while before I had to get ready for the game. Before I left, I gave him another hug and said, "I love you." Because I did. My heart absolutely went out to that kid the moment we met; his courage and spirit were incredible.

I set two ACC all-time records that day—career rushing touchdowns (50) and career total touchdowns (53)—and at the press conference afterward, Andrew fearlessly raised his hand alongside all the veteran journalists and media present. "Are those the best records you ever broke?" he asked.

"I think so," I told him. We both grinned at each other. I think he knew those records were his, too, because he helped inspire me to take the field that day with every ounce of strength and determination I had in me. Andrew's positivity was remarkable; he never complained about anything but did his best to absorb everything he could in each moment. His desire to be a part of things, despite his size and condition, was inspiring. Every movement he made was bursting with enthusiasm, as if he already understood, at five years old, the importance of attacking life with all you've got. As tiny as

Andrew was, everything about him was big: his grin, his excitement, his passion for sports, his love for his family. Although he was young, there was a wisdom in his eyes that let me know that by being there and encouraging me in his own special way, he was part of that game and, ultimately, part of my career.

When Andrew's mom asked him at home that night what he enjoyed most about his visit to Pitt, Andrew said that his favorite moment was meeting me: "I like that he had chemo like me. And he told me he loved me."

When I heard this, I was blown away. That kid worked his way into the heart of everyone on the sidelines that day, and yet he still felt a special connection with me because of what we had both been through. When he saw me, he knew he wasn't alone. I carefully signed one of my jerseys and sent it to him so that we could match on game day. I wanted Andrew to know that *I* knew we were part of each other's teams. Whatever inspiration I was supposed to have offered Andrew came back to me tenfold. When ESPN made a short documentary about my story and my inspiration called "For Those Who Can't," they asked about Andrew. I answered as honestly as I could: "That boy meant something in this world. He changed lives. He changed my life."

Just a few weeks after the game Andrew attended, I received the Disney Spirit Award, and, through my tears, I talked about Andrew, who was watching the program at home with this family. I explained how people like him inspire me to do something more with my second chance at my dreams and at life. I told the crowd, "There are people fighting and they don't get this, they don't receive any awards if they win and when they win, and so this is for all of us."

After my intense battle with Hodgkin's lymphoma, I knew I had a responsibility to do something with my second shot at life—something that would make it count not just for me but for everyone who would love to be where I now stand. I have the privilege to be where I am and the duty to make it matter. After experiencing all that cancer threw at me, I knew that everything I did—on the field and off—couldn't be just for myself or my own personal glory anymore. I want to honor everyone who has overcome their obstacles in addition to everyone who is still fighting their personal battles. It's an exhausting, sometimes soul-crushing journey to be in the midst of a serious diagnosis or life challenge, and by opening up about my story, I want to bring a little bit of light and hope to those who are fighting. I welcome anyone who feels a connection through our experiences because we really are all in this together.

I want to play for those who can't—for those people who may not ever be able to return to the field, the mat, or the pool because of their struggles. I was so lucky to be able to return to the sport I love—it's a gift that I didn't deserve any more than those who are still battling. These individuals are no less important than I am, but because I'm an NFL player, I get all the press and attention. With the platform I've been given, it's my duty to speak up for those who are still battling and those who have lost the battle—people like little Andrew O'Neil, who died four days after I received that award.

Second chances aren't guaranteed. I was incredibly blessed to get another shot at my dreams, but not everyone does. Throughout my journey, I have learned many things, but one of the most important is that my experiences don't just belong to me. Every victory I have ever enjoyed came about because God clearly saw that I still had a job to do here, and if I lose sight of that, I'm missing the point of everything else in life. If my victory over cancer was only intended for *me* to enjoy, what a small life that would be. The way I see it, any success I am enjoying now isn't just my own—it's something I share with everyone else who has faced a challenge that stole part of their dreams. As they see themselves in my story, and me in theirs, we all get to claim a part of the incredible things God has done for us and through us in our time on this earth.

I play for people like Ian Malesiewski, a kid from my hometown. A nationally ranked high school wrestler, he was also just an all-around great guy. The same day he took the mat to compete at the 2016 Greco-Roman Nationals in Akron, Ohio, Ian was reelected vice president of his class. By all counts, it should have been a perfect day for him. But it wasn't. As he fought his way out of a perfectly normal hold, he landed awkwardly and fractured two vertebrae in his neck. Ian is now paralyzed from the chest down.

His accident happened less than two weeks after I received the all clear on my health. Just as I was finally preparing to play the sport I loved again, Ian lost his dream. I met Ian that same summer and, as we became friends, I came face-to-face with a very difficult reality: there is no reason in the world why I should be able to compete while he is no longer able. I don't understand why things are the way they are—why I am able to run on a field and Ian can't walk onto a mat. I don't understand why it had to happen that way—why some people get to reclaim their dreams and others don't. It isn't fair, quite honestly. But I do know that my second chance is something I need to share. I want him to experience alongside me the excitement of athletic competition that we both love. My joy under the lights belongs to Ian, too.

I play for kids like Roman Pfister, another boy from my hometown. Roman had three open-heart surgeries before the age of six, and his biggest dream in life was to play football. Unfortunately, due to his condition, he can't play on a team, and his stadium will only ever be his backyard. But that doesn't mean he doesn't get his own touchdowns; it just means that I am the one scoring them for him. When Roman came to one of my games at Pitt, I spotted him on the sideline and gave him a huge hug. Afterward, I gave him a game ball and my game gloves, which he fell asleep wearing that night. Any victory I achieve on the field is part of my story, but it's also part of Roman's, too, because thinking of his enthusiasm and encouragement in the face of his own personal battles gives me the strength to keep pushing through, even on difficult days.

Any success I enjoy is also part of Chelsea's story, as I learned when she had the opportunity to attend one of our games after being diagnosed with a brain tumor. She was getting ready to start radiation therapy, and the game was one of her last big outings before her intensive treatments began. As I was leaving the field with my team after warm-ups, I heard someone say, "That's James Conner. You've got something in common with him."

I couldn't just walk on by after hearing that. "What do we have in common?" I asked as I turned around and smiled at the girl.

She looked surprised that I had stopped, but she said, "I have cancer."

"You've got this," I told her. We talked for a bit before I had to go into the locker room, but I hoped that when she saw me on the field later, she would know that the game wasn't just for me. I hoped she would know that when I pointed to the crowd, it was my way of saying, "This game belongs to you, too, because we are in this together."

Reagan, a fourteen-year-old who traveled all the way out from Utah as part of a Make-A-Wish Foundation wish grant, was excited for a break from her treatments to attend a Steelers game. After a jam-packed day full of visits and meeting new people, she was nervous and a little flustered when I came over to talk with her, so I just gave her a hug and whispered some encouragement to her. I understood how everything can just seem too much to take in. The most important thing to me was that she knew she wasn't alone; her fight is my fight, and my game is her game.

I play for kids like eleven-year-old Bray, from Ohio, who also has leukemia and whose wish was to attend the Pro Bowl. When his local paper asked him what he was excited about, he said, "Getting to meet James Conner . . . He's an NFL running back for the Steelers but a couple years ago, he had [cancer], too."

I'm in it for eighteen-year-old Thomas, too, who received the exact same diagnosis I did: stage II Hodgkin's lymphoma. When he came to watch my game, we talked about treatments and challenges, but we also talked about football and goals. And when I put on my helmet and laced up my cleats, I thought about how fortunate I was to be able to play for both myself *and* for Thomas—two guys with the same diagnosis and the same goals. I am just fortunate enough to be on the other side of my battle. But I never want to forget how overwhelming life can feel in the middle of it.

Every week at Pitt, the Make-A-Wish Foundation sponsored a different child to walk with the captains out to the middle of the field for the coin toss. My final year there, when I was on the other side of my own treatment, I walked with that child. It felt sacred to me, having that brave kid at my side. It didn't matter what condition he or she was facing, I knew we were united in our desire to make the most of our lives, to face our challenges with boldness, and to be the people God created us to be. They encourage me and make me stronger, and I hope I can do the same in return. We are part of the same team. When I invite other people to become part of my story, my success becomes that much bigger.

I've met so many wonderful kids through organizations like the Make-A-Wish Foundation and Children's Wish Foundation International, but I also know there are adults out there who I am playing for in a different way—people like Jonathan Smith. A lifelong Steelers fan, Jonathan wanted to take his two young boys to a game, but he was battling stage IV colon cancer and couldn't make the trip to the stadium. His boys went to a game with their aunt and got to go down on the sidelines to watch warm-ups; when I spotted them both wearing #30 jerseys, I knew I had to meet them. They told me about their family, and I gave them both high fives as we talked about their dad. I play for those boys, who still have their whole lives ahead of them to dream big dreams. I play for kids who wish they could be out there on the field, under the lights, in front of the cameras, doing something they love. But I also play for the dads and moms who would love to be able simply to run and play with their children in their own yard but can't because of a decline in health. I play for the people who are now counting life in months or weeks instead of years or decades.

I've really had to shift my thinking with regard to how I view time. I have always struggled with patience as far as my career is concerned; I used to wish for time to fly by until I made it to the next level. Since December 2015, I have come to learn that time is far too precious to wish away. Countless people would trade everything they own just for one more good day. After spending time with them, I see the naïveté of my old point of view. Don't get me wrong—it wasn't a quick or painless transformation, but it's been an important one. God forced me to have patience in my year of healing, but it didn't last long. The moment I got the all clear from Dr. Marks, I went tearing back into my final season at Pitt, ready to jump into my first season in the pros. But I had to be patient again—first on draft night and then again when it came to paying my dues. I was not the Steelers' starting running back; I still had a lot to learn about playing at the next level. I hate waiting, but I can also see the beauty of it, because waiting means that you still have time. Most important, though, I understand now that not everyone has that luxury. Not everyone has more time. Not everyone *can* wait. I eventually learned to thank God for whatever time I have, whatever form it takes.

I also thank God when he gives me a chance to prove what I can do with my second chance. When the 2018 season started and Le'Veon Bell decided not to take the field for the Steelers over contract issues, I suddenly found myself center stage in only my second season in the league. I had no idea how long the opportunity was going to last until Bell came back to play, but I knew I planned to make the most of it.

In our season opener against the Cleveland Browns on September 9, 2018, I racked up 31 carries for 135 rushing yards, the highest number in the entire NFL that week. With 11:16 left in the second quarter, I rushed for four yards into the end zone for my first NFL touchdown, carrying Andrew, Ian, and so many others with me over the line. Time stood still for just an instant and, for once, I didn't feel impatient. I knew that I was exactly where I wanted to be, here and now, in that moment—no rushing to accomplish the next thing. God had put me exactly where He wanted me: showing the world that hope is stronger than pain.

My season continued on a tear, as I remained in the starting running back position. It was as if all of the people for whom I was playing empowered me to take my game—our game—to a whole new level. In Week 8, I was named AFC Offensive Player of the Week along with AFC Offensive Player of the Month for October. I even cut my hair into a mullet as a humorous nod to my Yinzer (western Pennsylvanian) roots. The more ridiculous my hair became, the more fans loved it; we were all in on the joke, and I relished the feeling of community as we all celebrated great football together. Despite a leg injury against the Chargers that sidelined me for three weeks, I ended the season with 973 rushing yards, 12 rushing touchdowns, 55 receptions, 1 receiving touchdown, and 497 receiving yards.

Then, on December 18, the NFL named its Pro Bowl selections, and there was my name at running back. In just four years—almost to the day—I went from ACC Player of the Year to a torn MCL and cancer diagnosis to a Pro Bowler. The following summer, in the 2019 preseason, I was named to the NFL's annual top 100, a list voted on by fellow NFL players based on the previous season's performance. Talk about high mountain tops and deep, deep valleys.

But it is that first touchdown in Cleveland, on September 9, 2018, that will stay with me forever. For just a second or two, as my mind locked in the memory of that feeling, I knew that the joy of the moment had nothing to do with whether I physically beat cancer or not; it was that my illness had not succeeded in stealing my purpose.

Some people never make it to the other side of their illness; they never receive that call from their doctor telling them their body is free from whatever was limiting them. But that doesn't mean their disease won. As long as they keep on living the life they were meant to live—finding joy, loving the people around them, enjoying everything they can with the time they have left—that's victory.

Meeting these extraordinary kids has changed me, but I've been impacted even by people I have never met. I often have people reach out to me on behalf of someone else who is going through a challenging time or fighting through a difficult diagnosis. Not long ago, I sent a jersey and a good luck message to a young boy named Carter who was going through chemo; his uncle thanked me and sent me photos of Carter opening the package. The look of complete joy on his face was all I needed. I saved those photos to my phone, as I have many others, so I can open them up and remind myself of the amazing gift God has given me. Not only do I have a second chance, but I also have a second family of people whose stories are now part of mine. I play for all of them—the people I've been lucky enough to meet, the people I've connected with long-distance, and the people I don't know but who nevertheless see me on the field each Sunday and say, "James Conner is like me."

Now that I've got another shot at life, I want to make sure I do everything right—and a huge part of that is cheering on the people who are still in the middle of their own challenges. I want them to know that there is life not only on the other side of their obstacle but also right now, in the moment. Even—*especially*—if they can't do whatever it is that they love doing right now, I want to give them something to cheer for that represents all of us.

One of my favorite ways of doing that is when I partner with the University of Pittsburgh Medical Center for surprise visits to the Hillman Cancer Center facilities in the area. As I write this, in the past two weeks alone, we've visited three different hospitals that are part of the network to talk with patients and their families, connect with people who are struggling, and encourage anyone undergoing treatment. Those visits matter because they are one way I am able to let people know that I'm on their team.

In order to grow those relationships even more, I eventually want to launch a foundation. But to start, beginning with the 2019 season, I began hosting five cancer patients or survivors at each Steelers home game. I cover their travel costs and tickets to the game so that they can enjoy a day that honors all they are going through or all they have endured in the past. As long as I am active in the NFL, I will sponsor these trips because they are just one more way to build these connections and grow the network of people I carry with me every time I take the field. But, even more important, they are a way to build a family of support and encouragement for people who are going through one of the toughest challenges they will ever have to face. It's a way of bringing together a community where we all need each other.

I play for those who want to, who wish they could, who dream about it—but who aren't able to make it a reality. I play for those who can't. And this is where I have found my life's true significance—where God took my ambition of being a professional athlete and made it something so much bigger. Part of becoming "James Conner, football player and cancer survivor," was giving up my goal to be known only for my stats and on-field performance. As hard as it was for me to let go of that dream, I now see how limited it really was.

My personal gifts were given to me by God, which means I have a responsibility to use them for His glory. A huge part of that is bringing hope and encouragement to other people who have faced similar struggles, and I am grateful for the way He created me for that purpose. I am not a huge extrovert, but I do love connecting with people on a personal level, something God has used to help me grow in empathy. As much as I love the peaks in my life, when everything is going great, I can now see how God also uses the valleys to shape us into the people He wants us to be. He used my lowest points to refine me, reshape me, and rejuvenate me. He changed my personal ambitions to make them for a larger purpose, to re-arrange my viewpoint to encompass more than just myself. I don't spend hours practicing my craft in order to be a celebrity. I don't take the field each week because I'm driven by a paycheck. I play because I know there are people out there who can't, and God gifted me with the opportunity to share something that feels like it be-longs to us all. Sports offer that kind of unity, after all, in the way they bring people together on the field, in the stands, and watching at home. I am deeply grateful that God has blessed me with a career that unifies people.

Whatever you have been through in life, whatever you are facing, know that you are going through it for a reason that is bigger than your own story. When you use your talents to honor those who can't and serve others, you set an example for those who would love to be in your shoes. Your courage to engage life with passion and chase your dreams despite setbacks sends a message to others. By coming out on the other side of a challenging time stronger than ever, you are carrying a little bit of their fear and discouragement; you are making their load a little lighter because they know you've already walked this road. You've faced the worst and made it past, and now you get to join the crowd of people cheering them on from the other side of that pain.

I never would have chosen to go through what I did, but I wouldn't change it for anything because it brought me to where I am now and to every place I will ever go. My ordeal shaped me in ways I never imagined I might have needed, but now I can see it has made me a much more grateful and humble person. Even my bad days now just feel like a little blip because I know I have been through worse and still survived. Whatever inconvenience I'm facing now is nothing compared to what God has already walked through with me. I have been deeply blessed because of my cancer, which feels like a very strange thing to write, and definitely not something I would have said when I first received the diagnosis. But I have seen the way God worked through it not only to make me a better man but also to give me a broader purpose.

Not everyone gets to run down that tunnel, see the lights, hear the roar of thousands of screaming fans as their feet hit the turf. Unfortunately, life steals a lot of dreams from people for a lot of different reasons. We've all had to let go of a vision of ourselves that we cherished, and it's never easy. Sometimes it's because of an illness or an injury; other times, it's a challenging circumstance or just the passage of time. When I was drafted, my brothers told me, "This is the greatest moment of our lives." They loved playing, but they never had the opportunity to go to this big of a stage. Their stories took different paths. But they live that dream with me each time I strap on that helmet. So did Andrew. So do Ian, Roman, and all the other amazing fans I have been privileged to meet. I understand how blessed I am, and I will make this second chance at football, and at life, count—for me, for them, and for us.

I was given a second chance to chase my dreams with just as much focus and drive as before—only this time, I'm determined to do something different. This time, I'm bringing people along with me. The friendships I've made as a result of my very public battle with cancer have become an essential part of who I am. I carry many of those friends and their stories with me as we go through life together. A piece of their story becomes a piece of mine, and a piece of mine becomes theirs. And now, I hope, a piece of that story will become yours, too.

All of us—you, me, the kids I meet, the patients who find hope in #30, the people who are still pushing their way through their darkest hours—are united not by what we have endured but by the spirit with which we fought through it, no matter the outcome.

As you shape your destiny every day, you have a choice to make as to how you are going to live your life. Choose joy. Perspective. Humility. Trust. Patience. Endurance. Encouragement. Faith. Hope. Love.

Choose anything but fear.

ACKNOWLEDGMENTS

I want to extend my sincerest thanks to everyone who made this project possible, because it was no small undertaking to write a book in the midst of training and editing it during the season!

First of all, I want to thank my family, who were willing to sit down for hours of interviews and answer lots of texts as we re-created all the details of my journey. To Glen, Richard, and Michael, thanks for pitching in yet again to help your baby brother do something awesome. To my dad, Glen — thank you for modeling hard work and devotion to your family. I owe a special thanks to my mom, Kelly, because I know it wasn't easy to have to relive some of the darkest days of my diagnosis and treatment. But she was there for me as I lived it, and she was there for me as I wrote about it, because that's the kind of amazing woman she is.

I am incredibly grateful to the Steelers coaching staff, my teammates, and the entire organization for the support and encouragement as I worked to share my story with fans. I am incredibly proud to be part of such an incredible team under the leadership of Head Coach Mike Tomlin and part of such a beautiful and enthusiastic community that is the Steeler Nation.

The faculty and staff of the University of Pittsburgh — especially the athletic department — are the most dynamic and dedicated group of individuals I know. Thank you to everyone who went the extra mile for me both when I was a student and while I was writing this book: Coach Pat Narduzzi, Coach Paul Chryst, Coach Andre Powell, Rob Blanc, E. J. Borghetti, and so many more people that I can't even name you all. The same is true of my amazing teammates who kept me going even on days when I wasn't sure I had it in me to take one more step. From the bottom of my heart, thank you.

I want to thank everyone who made time to talk with me and with Tiffany: Sean, Carson, Coach Soboleski, Coach Spooner. You all are such a huge part of who I am and the story I have to tell.

I will never be able to express fully my respect for and appreciation of everything the healthcare team at the University of Pittsburgh Medical Center and the Hillman Cancer Center, specifically, did and continue to do for me and countless other patients. Dr. Stanley Marks, Dr. Robert Ferris, the wonderful nurses and support staff who greet me every visit, the PR team that arranged for us to tour the facilities and conduct interviews while writing this book— thank you for everything you do, every day. You are the best team anyone could ask for.

To my incredible team at HarperCollins, including our fantastic editor Eric Nelson and deputy publisher Doug Jones, who really advocated for this book in the first place — thank you so, so much for believing in me. I am deeply grateful for the chance to share more of my journey with the world.

ACKNOWLEDGMENTS

To Karl Roser, the Steelers photographer who also loaned his tremendous talents to this project, thank you for making me look better every single time you snap your camera!

To Nima Zarrabi, my manager, and Ryan Tollner, my sports agent, you stood by me when no other agents did, and I will be forever grateful for that.

To Cassie Hanjian, my literary agent who had a vision for this book and who represented it *like an absolute boss*, thank you for recognizing the potential in my story and being such a vocal supporter throughout this entire process. This book wouldn't have happened without you.

To my co-writer, Tiffany Yecke Brooks, thank you for all of the time you invested interviewing the people who know my story best and for the tireless hours you put into helping me tell my story in the most authentic and meaningful way possible. I hope you are as proud of what we created here as I am.

And finally, to everyone who has walked or is walking the cancer walk — or, really, any difficult journey — thank you for picking up this book. Thank you for listening to what I had to say. Thank you for being part of my team and for allowing me to be part of yours. Whatever happens, just know that I'm in your corner, and fear is a choice.

ABOUT THE AUTHORS

James Conner is a running back for the Pittsburgh Steelers. In his freshman year at the University of Pittsburgh, James ran for 229 yards to break Tony Dorsett's school record for most rushing yards in a bowl game. The following year, James set an ACC record with 26 rushing touchdowns in one season and was named ACC Player of the Year. He made a triumphant return his senior year, propelling him into the NFL, where he was named to the Pro Bowl for the 2018 season.

Tiffany Yecke Brooks has worked as a lead or contributing writer for more than two dozen books. She holds a PhD in literature from Florida State University and teaches writing and publishing courses at several universities.